MARCO ⊕ POLO
MEXICO

with Local Tips
*The author's special recommendations are
highlighted in yellow throughout this guide*

P9-CPV-875

There are five symbols to help you find your way around this guide:

★

Marco Polo's top recommendations – the best in each category

sites with a scenic view

places where the local people meet

places where young people get together

(150/A1)
pages and coordinates for the Road Atlas of Mexico
(U/A1) *coordinates for the City Map of Mexico City inside back cover*
(O) *area not covered by the City Map*

MARCO ⊕ POLO

Travel guides and language guides in this series:

Algarve • Amsterdam • Australia/Sydney • Berlin • Brittany • California
Canada • Channel Islands • Costa Brava/Barcelona • Costa del Sol/Granada
Côte d'Azur • Crete • Cuba • Cyprus • Dominican Republic • Eastern Canada
Eastern USA • Florence • Florida • Gran Canaria • Greek Islands/Aegean
Ibiza • Ireland • Istanbul • Lanzarote • London • Mallorca • Malta • Mexico
New York • New Zealand • Normandy • Paris • Prague • Rhodes • Rome
Scotland • South Africa • Southwestern USA • Tenerife • Turkish Coast
Tuscany • Venice • Western Canada

French • German • Italian • Spanish

*Marco Polo would be very interested to hear your
comments and suggestions. Please write to:*

North America:
Marco Polo North America
70 Bloor Street East
Oshawa, Ontario, Canada
(B) 905-436-2525

United Kingdom:
GeoCenter International Ltd
The Viables Centre
Harrow Way
Basingstoke, Hants RG22 4BJ

*Our authors have done their research very carefully, but should any errors or omissions
have occurred, the publisher cannot be held responsible for any injury, damage
or inconvenience suffered due to incorrect information in this guide*

Cover photograph: Focus/Joe McNally
Photos: author (30, 100); A. M. Gross (22); HB-Verlag (8, 55, 57, 63, 67, 70, 89, 94, 107, 108, 111);
Heck (19); R. Kiedrowski (60); Lade: Berer (86), Welsh (7); Mauritius: Fichtl (133), Fischer (136), fm (92),
Gebhardt (12, 41), Günther (14), Höbel (16, 29), Hubatka (149), Kuhn (83), Murillo (114), Pigneter (135),
Schmied (126), Thonig (47, 103), Torino (4, 24, 64, 78, 80, 97, 119, 120), Vidler (33, 48, 68);
Schuster: Prisma (98); Transglobe: List (26), Riethmüller (37); Zawodsky-Foto (20)

1ˢᵗ edition 2000
© Mairs Geographischer Verlag, Ostfildern, Germany
Author: Manfred Rohlf
Translator: Dennis Brehme
English edition 2000: Gaia Text
Editorial director: Ferdinand Ranft
Chief editor: Marion Zorn
Cartography for the Road Atlas: © Mairs Geographischer Verlag
Design and layout: Thienhaus/Wippermann
Printed in Germany

CONTENTS

Discover Mexico!

*The country of three cultures lures the visitor
with its snow-capped volcanoes, colossal pyramids
and Baroque churches*

Cantinas and haciendas, glistening bays and magnificent, wide beaches bordered by graceful palm trees, chic coastal resorts and hammock get-togethers for part-time hippies, elegant palaces decorated with stucco and the most opulent Baroque, seven-storeyed pyramids boasting a jaguar throne, an exciting folklore and Indian heritage: not without reason is Mexico one of the most popular tourist destinations in the world. In spite of its continuing popularity, Mexico is so big that the visitor never feels that the country has been taken over by tourism. There are exceptions, though, such as in Acapulco, where one high-rise hotel after another line the beaches, and in Cancún, where mass tourism really gets going. Those who go there enjoy the feeling of being part of the hustle and bustle, seeking the countless discos, restaurants and sporting clubs to find amusement.

The 365 steps of the 'El Castillo' pyramid in Chichén Itzá represent the days of the year

Admittedly, in a country as huge and varied as Mexico, there are still many small and secluded bays perfect for swimming, sunbathing and relaxing — and, with the two wonderful tropical coasts of the Pacific Ocean and the Caribbean Sea, there are more than 10,000 km of magnificent coastline.

The classical resorts of the Pacific coast were known to Hollywood film stars and wealthy Americans as early as the 1940s, but they certainly looked different back then. When Errol Flynn came to Acapulco for the first time in 1942, there wasn't much of a city, but the beautiful, empty sandy beaches and graceful palm trees were certainly alluring. The now famous small harbour of Puerto Vallarta north of Acapulco became well known only when the Tennessee Williams play 'The Night of the Iguana' was made into a film starring Richard Burton and Ava Gardner in 1964. To ensure that Richard behaved well, his wife Liz Taylor came along, who was so captivated by the tropical landscape that she had a house built in the so-called 'Gringo's Gully'.

History at a glance

7000–2500 BC
Hunters and gatherers inhabit the area; the ancestors of the Maya live in present-day Guatemala

800 BC
Olmecs build the first pyramid

AD 250–900
The Classic age of the Mayan civilization in Mexico; about AD 900, the Maya mysteriously abandon their city states

6th century
Heyday of the Totonaca capital of El Tajín

9th century
The Toltec capital of Tula is founded; the emergence of roofed structures supported by massive columns

14th century
The Aztecs found the city of Tenochtitlán and conquer other Indian peoples as far away as Guatemala

1519
Hernán Cortés lands on the coast near Veracruz in the Gulf of Mexico

1521
Cortés conquers Tenochtitlán; 100,000 Aztecs lose their lives

1521–45
Conquest and Christianization: Mexico becomes New Spain, many colonial cities are founded

Until 1810
The Indian population is decimated by smallpox, from approx. 20 to 3 million; mineral resources are shipped to Spain

1810
The priest Miguel Hidalgo proclaims Mexico's independence; a ten-year-long War of Independence ensues

1821
Mexico becomes an independent country, two years later a federal republic

1846–48
In the Mexican-American War, Mexico cedes Upper California, Arizona and New Mexico (Texas had been ceded in 1836)

1876–1911
Dictatorship of Porfirio Díaz

1910
Francisco Madero starts the Mexican Revolution to overthrow Díaz; soon, Pancho Villa and Emiliano Zapata join the revolutionary forces

1917
Towards the end of the civil war, a new Constitution is adopted

1929–40
Land reforms

1976
Large crude oil deposits are found in the Gulf of Mexico

1985
The worst earthquake in Mexican history strikes the capital

1998
In the as yet unresolved conflict between the government and the Zapatistas and their Indian supporters, the federal powers refuse to comply with the agreements reached in 1996 and reject the intervention of a mediator

Whereas the Pacific coastline is solely for bathing and relaxing on the beach, that of the Caribbean offers cultural and historical sites as well, as many Mayan ruins of the Yucatán Peninsula are only a short drive away from the resorts.

On the other side of the country, the 1,300-km-long and on the average only 90-km-wide peninsula of Baja California, geographically speaking an extension of California, still remains relatively empty and unexplored. This dry peninsula branches off the Mexican mainland in its extreme north, jutting out into the Pacific Ocean and creating the Gulf of California in the process. Crystalline water, hidden sandy coves and rugged cliffs characterize this impressive coastal landscape. Right behind the few hotels on the coast, and sometimes reached by primitive gravel roads, lies the ageless, magnificent desert landscape, away from all civilization.

Apart from the tropical sandy beaches, it is the country's rich pre-Columbian past that attracts visitors. Countless archaeological sites, many 1,000 to 2,000 years old, have been excavated and saved from the encroaching jungle vegetation. On the Yucatán Peninsula, the Mayan ruins of Cobá, situated deep in the jungle and surrounded by five lakes, captivate the imagination of every tourist. If that were not enough, the ruined city of Tulum, south of Cancún, offers perhaps the world's most spectacular setting, with its temples built on top of high cliffs overlooking the turquoise waters of the Caribbean Sea. And the opposite can also be found: high above the clouds, in the interior, lies Monte Albán

The Bay of Mismaloya: the scene of many Hollywood movies

overlooking the Valley of Oaxaca. In order to build this amazing ceremonial centre to honor the Indian gods, an entire hilltop was painstakingly levelled. Closer to Tulum, the world-famous Mayan ruins of Chichén Itzá provide a unique spectacle every equinox: the shadow thrown by the sun moves up the pyramid of 'El Castillo', giving the impression that a giant serpent is slowly moving up to the top.

The first-time visitor to Mexico should plan his or her trip carefully. There are so many different landscapes, racial groups and cultural remains that it is not advisable to try to see it all in just a few weeks. Mexico has an enormous variety of sights in a huge area — with its two million square kilometres and a north-south expanse of more than 3,000 km, it is roughly eight times larger than the UK. This impressive size means plenty of opportunity for everyone to discover his or her own Mexico.

Mexico City, for example: the chaotic, earthquake-prone and

hopelessly overpopulated metropolis of 25 million, full of honking cars and smog. This is the city Mexicans themselves describe as the most Mexican of all. Some discover a highly sophisticated and cosmopolitan world capital full of palaces, museums and theatres, while others value the city's countless elegant gourmet restaurants and the old haciendas converted into luxurious first-class hotels, where the visitor has the feeling of living in another century. Others love the loud, colourful Mexico of the street vendors and hot food stalls, of the travelling entertainers of Alameda Park, and the *mariachi* bands on the Plaza of Garibaldi.

On almost every corner of this giant metropolis, the visitor finds historical traces of a glorious past. In the Palacio Nacional, for example, where the Mexican president has his office, one can admire the greatest masterpieces of Diego Rivera (1886–1957). His largest work occupies the entire wall next to the stairwell leading to the upper floor: *Epic of the Mexican People* — a monumental fresco, called a *mural* by Mexicans, in which Rivera portrays the most important turning points in post-Columbian Mexican history. Not far from the Colonial splendour of the National Palace lie the remains of the enormous Templo Mayor, the biggest ceremonial temple of the Aztec capital of Tenochtitlán, destroyed by Cortés in 1521.

History is so pervasive in Mexico that the visitor finds it in the most unlikely places, even while having a drink or enjoying a meal — in the Bar Opera, for example, where the most important personalities of the Mexican Revolution once dined. It is assumed that the hole seen in the yellowed ceiling of the bar came from Pancho Villa's revolver. And in the southern part of the city, dictator Porfirio Díaz was a regular weekend guest of the former country estate Antigua Hacienda de Tlalpan.

Mexico City offers a unique opportunity to study all of the coun-

Showplace of the capital: the huge Zócalo in Mexico City

try's varied social classes. In the busy intersections of the principal avenues, one can see small children performing their acrobatic numbers or tricks in front of waiting cars. Others clean the windshields or sell lottery tickets for a few pesos in the precious few minutes allowed by the red light. This hard-earned money forms an important part in the subsistence of their large families. In the city centre, at the Zócalo opposite the giant cathedral, one can see day after day unemployed tradesmen patiently waiting to be hired — for one single day or just a few hours. Farther north, on Sundays, faithful Catholics can be seen approaching the Basilica of the Virgin of Guadalupe on their knees. The most worshipped saint is dark-skinned; at least here, Mexicans of all social classes intermingle freely, there are no racial differences in the nation's most important place of pilgrimage. A world away is the Pink Zone, or Zona Rosa, with its exclusive boutiques and high-heeled, smartly dressed señoritas window-shopping or meeting their friends or relatives in one of the popular European-style restaurants. A few paces away, humble shoe-cleaners hope to earn a few pesos for their services from the wealthy restaurant clients, native or foreign.

To get an impression of Mexico's varied landscape, it is recommended to tour the country. The public transportation system is highly efficient; coaches connect remote towns and cities with one another. The old railway system takes its time to do the same, and for those in a hurry, the small domestic airlines do their job quite well. On trips through the country, it's often not even necessary to take one's own lunch, as Mexican housewives offer the typical *tacos* filled with chicken. But beware, it can be 'muy picante, señor!' (hot and spicy). Other offerings are coconut cakes (home-baked, of course) and fresh oranges. Children offer Coca-Cola, which is then poured into a cup and sipped through a straw. Nowhere else does the visitor get such a good impression of the country than in these journeys through the countryside.

In the dry north, cacti and thornbrush steppes characterize the vegetation. The greener south boasts tropical rain forests and impassable jungles. The Sierra Madre Occidental and the Sierra Madre Oriental run from north to south, their high peaks visible from the coast. In the high mountains, magnificent oak and pine forests can be seen among the canyons. The biggest of all, the Copper Canyon (Barranca del Cobre) is deeper than its counterpart, the Grand Canyon. This is still the home of pumas, bears and wolves. Few people live here. The Tarahumara Indians are the only ones who have managed to survive in this harsh environment.

Snow-capped volcanoes dot the central highlands. It is here where most Mexicans live, in the valleys and highlands created by the Sierra Volcánica Transversal, the country's largest volcanic mountain range. Earthquakes are natural occurrences here, and as long as they're not too severe, nobody is afraid of them. It is also here where the visitor finds the greatest number of unforgettable colonial cities. The most magnif-

9

icent colonial Baroque can be found within a radius of only several hundred kilometres away from the capital. Around the central *plaza* of every town they founded, the Spaniards erected a church and the most important public buildings, such as the city hall and the hospital. The cobbled streets were laid out like a grid and lined with one- or two-storeyed houses with flat roofs, massive wooden doors and wrought-iron bars in front of the windows. The rather plain-looking houses offer a very different view inside, where the owner can really show off. An oasis of tranquillity is the patio. In the middle of this inner courtyard bordered by arcades, there is always a fountain decorated by the artistic creations of stonemasons, and the splashing of water is a welcome, soothing sound. The many flowers of this interior garden exude their fragrance and the trees provide welcome shade. Since many colonial houses have been converted into hotels in recent times, the visitor can also partake in the beauty and atmosphere of colonial architecture.

The victorious Spaniards lost no time decorating the churches in the most luxurious way possible. They then proceeded to import the most lavishly deco-rated Baroque, the Churrigueresque style, from Spain. The church interiors were soon filled with hundreds of little angels, saints, leaves and flowers, in some cases with figures from Indian mythology, and all covered with gold leaf. Some of the best examples of this architectural style can be admired in the cities located along the 'Route of the Independence': Guanajuato, San Miguel de Allende and Querétaro, which by the way also witnessed some of the fiercest battles of the War of Independence. The history museums housed in their city halls vividly portray the long and bloody road to freedom.

Mexico's powerful neighbour to the north, the USA, pervades the life in northern Mexico, especially in the border cities. Here, the 'American way of life' has moved in: the cities are newer, the streets wider, many signs have American names, hamburgers and chips are sold everywhere, and many men don't call themselves Carlos but Charlie instead. Many already work for the numerous American and multinational companies that have established assembly plants along the border. Tijuana, across the border from San Diego, is the city that has the highest number of visitors, and it has made an industry out of border tourism. This amusement metropolis offers mostly gambling dens, pubs, restaurants serving *Tex-Mex food* and souvenir shops. Although many Americans cross the border to get a glimpse of the culture, Tijuana is as Mexican as Hong Kong is Chinese. In spite of the orientation towards the American way of life, Mexicans in general have a strained and ambivalent relationship towards the *gringos*, as Americans are called here. Mexicans appreciate very much if the visitor makes an effort to communicate in Spanish, rather than assume that all Mexicans understand and speak fluent English.

Even though Mexicans are difficult to characterize, many attempts have nevertheless been made to do so. The best are by Octavio Paz, the 1990 winner of the Nobel Prize for Literature. In his famous collection of essays titled 'The Labyrinth of Solitude', Paz eloquently describes the differences between Mexicans and the powerful northern neighbours: 'The North Americans are credulous and we are believers; they love fairy tales and detective stories and we love myths and legends; we get drunk in order to confess, they get drunk in order to forget. They are optimists and we are nihilists – except that our nihilism is not intellectual but instinctive, and therefore irrefutable. We are suspicious and they are trusting. We are sorrowful and sarcastic and they are happy and full of jokes. North Americans want to understand and we want to contemplate. They are activists and we are quietists; we enjoy our wounds and they enjoy their inventions. They believe in hygiene, health, work and contentment, but perhaps they have never experienced true joy, which is an intoxication, a whirlwind. In the hubbub of a fiesta night our voices explode into brilliant lights, and life and death mingle together, while their vitality becomes a fixed smile that denies old age and death, but that changes life to motionless stone.'

Mexico is the nation of three cultures. In Tlatelolco, a neighbourhood of Mexico City, on the Plaza de las Tres Culturas, the silent witnesses of the most important epochs of Mexican history can all be seen together: the remains of pre-Columbian temples, a 16th-century church built by the Spaniards and the most modern 20th-century buildings, among them the present Ministry of Foreign Affairs. Inscribed on a plaque can be read: 'On 13 August 1521, Hernán Cortés conquered Tlatelolco, so valiantly held by Cuauhtémoc. This was neither a victory nor a defeat, but the painful birth of Mexico and of its mestizo peoples.' In the church La Concepción, at the Plaza de la Concepción Tequipeuca, another inscription offers a different view: 'Tequipeuhcan – the place where slavery began. Emperor Cuauhtémoc was taken prisoner in the afternoon of 13 August 1521.'

The beginning of slavery or the birth of the Mexican people? From the collision of radically different cultures and peoples and over the course of many centuries, the society of modern Mexico has emerged.

From Frida Kahlo to the cult of the dead

When can one eat the delicious skulls made from chocolate?
Where do tapir and raccoon say good night to each other?
Who flies 30 metres above the ground?

Population

The conquest of Mexico by Hernán Cortés in 1521 was the birth of the Mexican people, since it marked the start of the racial mixing of Indians and Spaniards, a gradual process that took place over many centuries. Nowadays, approximately 80 per cent of all Mexicans are classified as mestizos (mixed), and only 15 per cent of the population is of pure Indian descent, the direct descendants of Cuauhtémoc, the last proud Aztec emperor. Often, the pure Indian can be distinguished from the mestizo only by his elaborate and colourful costume. The best known of all the numerous Indian communities are the descendants of the Aztecs living in the central highlands and the two-million-strong Maya of southern Mexico. The visitor will run into other Indian groups, however, such as the Totonacs (seeing them perform their high-flying act) as *voladores* as well as the Tarascan Indians selling

The famous Calendar Stone of the Aztecs can be admired in Mexico City

their wares in the markets of western Mexico. Once the rulers of their own country, the Indians are now the poorest of the poor. On the highest economic stratum are the *criollos*, the white descendants of the Spaniards and other whites, who make out approximately 5 per cent of the population.

In early 1994, unrest began in the southernmost state of Chiapas when an Indian guerilla force occupied several towns for a short period. The rebels call themselves *Ejército Zapatista de Liberación Nacional* (EZLN), 'The Zapatista National Liberation Army'. Their main purpose was to protest against the prevailing social misery in the state and particularly against the extreme poverty of the Indian population (such as the Lacandons, whose lands were taken from them and are now in the hands of a few big landowners). The men find their inspiration in the motto *tierra y libertad* ('Land and Freedom') coined by the legendary revolutionary Emiliano Zapata in 1910. A considerable share of the inhabitants of Chiapas think that the revolt is justified and supports it, so that the countermeasures taken by the authorities haven't made much headway. The conflict couldn't be solved by former President Salinas de Gortari, and so far his successor Ernesto Zedillo hasn't made much progress, either. The bishop of San Cristóbal de las Casas was able to ease the conflict somewhat, but it continues to smolder and flare up once in a while. The federal government and the representatives of the rebels keep negotiating, but a solution hasn't been achieved. Tourism in the region suffered at first, but has since recovered.

Mexico presently has 95 million people, and approximately one-fourth of them live in and around the capital. The metropolis keeps growing as long as the emigration to the cities continues. Mexico is a young country: about one-half of the population is under 20 years of age. If the population continues to increase as quickly as it has, then there will be well over 100 million Mexicans in the new millennium. In the overcrowded cities, a small middle and upper class face a large, impoverished and growing lower class. This state of affairs will continue as long as the high inflation and falling agricultural prices force more and more *campesinos*, farmers and agricultural workers, into poverty. Since much of the land is not arable, it doesn't even yield enough for the self-subsistence of the farmers' large families. Many have no choice but to emigrate to the cities, where jobs are few and far between – ideally, every year the Mexican economy should create 800,000 jobs – but since this doesn't happen, the emigrants join the frustrated, young masses that desperately try to earn a meagre living in the crime-infested shantytowns on the outskirts of cities. As poor as they are, there's always enough money to purchase a television set: the programmes give them a taste of a world that will always be out of reach; a similar escape from the harsh everyday reality is provided by numerous comics.

Flora and fauna

The amazing variety seen in Mexico's landscape is home to an immense wealth of plant species. You can find everything, from European-looking fir and pine forests in western Mexico to tropical rain forests where precious hardwoods and countless orchids grow. Even in the semi-arid highlands, bougainvilleas, hibiscus and magnolias provide swabs of colour in the brown landscape. Mexico boasts 25,000 different flowering plants, and everywhere you look there are endless varieties of cacti. Of the endemic species, the one that visitors ad-

The cactus: deserts of Baja California are typical of the barren beauty of the arid north

mire most is the colossal candelabrum cactus, which can grow to truly gigantic proportions.

The mostly inaccessible gorges of the Sierra Madre provide shelter for black bears, coyotes, foxes, beavers and wild boars. In the low-lying areas, jaguars, pumas and countless monkeys still abound. In addition, badgers, otters, lynx, ocelots, tapirs, raccoons, deer and armadillos can be found. Birds with iridescent feathers are often seen, the most beautiful of which are the parrots and hummingbirds. The coastal regions are the playground of pelicans and flamingos, herons and cormorants, geese and ducks. As if that were not enough, the waters off the Caribbean teem with tropical fish of all sizes and colours. In addition, Mexico has the greatest number of reptile species and is second in the number of mammals and fourth in amphibians.

Women

In the land of machos, women have a hard time: they earn only a fraction of what men earn and a disproportionate number of them work in the lowest jobs. Although divorced men are forced by law to support their families, many just disappear, forcing the women and their children to struggle on their own to make a living. In macho society, a golden ring on a woman's finger counts more than the best mark in school, and only women who bear many sons are given a higher status.

Admittedly, there is a world of difference between those women who live in decrepit adobe huts, facing the daily struggle of existence and those who lead comfortable, carefree lives in the elegant suburbs, with maids and a chauffeur. What the visitor immediately notices is that the economic status of Mexican women can readily be seen in the clothes and make-up they wear. The higher the social class, the more expensive the make-up and the manicure. Only seldom is a Mexican woman dressed casually. Even on very hot days women wear stockings and tight skirts, and high-heeled shoes are always a must. Thus, in a macho society, it's only natural for women to be taught early on to cater to the tastes of men; many Mexican men are filled with pride when the eyes of male passersby approvingly rest for a short time on their female companions.

Women live in their own world. Their preferred communication partners are not their husbands, as might be expected, but primarily their mothers, female friends and neighbours. The working world of Mexican women depends solely on the age and social class of the husband. In the lower classes, the older daughters look after their younger brothers and sisters while the mother is at work. Owing to the high rate of unemployment and the often inadequate education of Mexican women, many are forced to work in the informal sector, for example as maids or street vendors selling hot food.

Frida Kahlo

Pablo Picasso was enthusiastic about her paintings; Marcel Duchamp and André Breton were some of her admirers. At the early age of 31, she enjoyed great success

Mariachi players are the embodiment of Mexican folklore

in the USA, and even far-away Europe has now discovered her. Nevertheless, as long as she lived, she painted in the shadow of her famous husband, Diego Rivera, whom she married twice. While Rivera's monumental frescoes decorated many public buildings in Mexico (and even some in the USA), she preferred to withdraw to her small studio, where she painted small canvases, mostly self-portraits revealing the sorrow and lifelong pain she had to endure as a consequence of an accident she had in 1925, when she was only 18. She was operated on many times, and towards the end of her life, one of her legs even had to be amputated, forcing her to continue painting from a wheelchair. All her life, she remained loyal to her two passions: Diego and painting. She passed away in 1954 and has since then become an inter-national cult figure.

Agriculture

After the Mexican Revolution was triggered by the demand for *tierra y libertad* ('Land and Freedom'), the new Constitution of 1917 included a law for the re-distribution of private land, to be given to landless farmers *(peones)*. Larger estates were then run as state-owned farms. Since then, the extensive land redistribution has come to a standstill and only a partial solution to this endless problem has been achieved, as there are still countless farmers waiting for their plot of land, but there is no more land to go around. Some farmers complain that the land given to them is so bad that it can't be used for farm-ing and as a consequence, many live below the poverty line. It's only through the cultivation of maize and beans that they can barely survive. In order to achieve self-subsistence with maize and grain, extensive agricultural de-veloping plans have been drawn up. However, funds for the nec-essary infrastructure (irrigation, etc.) are often insufficient, so the dire situation of the farmer is not likely to change in the near future.

Mariachi music

You should dedicate one evening in Mexico City to Plaza Garibaldi, the meeting place of numerous *mariachi* bands. *Mariachis* — the name probably derives from the French word 'mariage' for marriage, which is still the golden opportunity for every *mariachi* group to show off — can consist of up to ten musicians, including the lead singer. They are easy to find, in their elegant attire: black suits with delicate and expensive silver embroidery and the characteristic broad-brimmed hats. Included in their repertoire are romantic-melancholic Mexican folk songs ardently performed by the group and accompanied by violins, trumpets and guitars. The proud musicians work only when their services are needed, playing for couples in love or for tourists. In restaurants, they can make an evening truly unforgettable.

The Maya

One and a half millennia ago, the main area of influence of the Mayan civilization was the Yucatán Peninsula and Guatemala. The intelligent Maya stood out from the rest of the Mesoamerican cultures particularly for developing a complex calendar and writing system. The 'rhythm of time became an obsession for them; the unending stream of passing days originating from the eternity of the past moving to the eternity of the future filled them with awe' as lifelong Mayan expert Thompson has described their thinking. To mark the passing of time, large steles and altars were erected; priests calculated the revolutions of Venus in the firmament and predicted solar eclipses with stunning accuracy. They used a vigesimal system (based on the number 20) and introduced zero in their calculations centuries before the Europeans did.

In order to document important events, astronomical calculations and rituals for their descendants, the Maya developed highly complex hieroglyphs, many chiselled in stone. In addition, they used long handwritten paper scrolls as books, also known as codices. Sadly, the great majority of them did not survive the Spanish conquest, as they were systematically burned by the Spaniards. It doesn't seem to amaze the visitor and archaeologist that this highly advanced civilization didn't use the potter's wheel or the wheel (which by the way was known to them and has been found in children's toys). In architecture, instead of the true vault they used the false or corbelled vault: a series of stones from opposite sides of a wall were placed in such a way that each one projected slightly beyond the one below until one single stone was enough to close the vault. In the heyday of their civilization, between the 4th and 9th centuries AD, numerous city-states were founded deep in the tropical rain forest. Pyramids and temples were carefully built and accurately aligned with one another; their perfect planning doesn't cease to amaze us. Many aspects of Mayan culture (and pre-Columbian civilizations in general) are explained and described in the lavishly illustrated book *The Art of Mesoamerica* by Mary Ellen Miller (Thames & Hudson), an inexpensive, large-format paperback volume.

Bullfighting

…and on Sundays we go to the bullfight, one of the most popular pastimes for young and old, families and couples in love. The popularity of this bloody spectacle introduced by the Spaniards in 1526 is still undiminished. In the mid-19th century, President Benito Juárez prohibited the spectacle, but his successor Porfirio Díaz lifted the ban only a few years later. Others have tried to do away with it, but without success, the *corrida de toros* has remained popular to the present day. The world's biggest bull ring is in Mexico City. The season runs from November to April, and the bullfights usually begin at 4 pm every Sunday afternoon (since this coincides with the dry season, no rain is expected). The spectators expect six fights, each one divided into *tercios*, or three acts.

The cult of the dead

Those who have the good fortune to be in Mexico in late October or early November can witness this bizarre and, for European eyes, rather macabre but uniquely Mexican spectacle, the *día de los muertos*, the Day of the Dead, when Mexicans believe that the souls of the dead come to their homes to pay them a visit. For many, this is the most important day of the year, and preparations start many weeks in advance. Shopkeepers make room for the many indispensable props: ceramic and papier-mâché skulls, groups of skeletons playing music, miniature cardboard coffins that open up to reveal a corpse (perhaps bearing your name?), life-size skeletons placed before entrances. The bakeries try to outdo each other: each one proudly advertises its wares by painting the windows with graveyard scenes; inside, garish, sugared skulls with the names of the living iced on to the forehead are eagerly bought by customers (especially children); chocolate-covered skulls and marzipan coffins are also quite popular.

When the significant evening finally arrives, many candles are lit in all houses and along the paths leading to the graveyards, so the spirits of the dead can find their way. Inside the houses, an altar for the dead is set up in a room, which is decorated with flowers (especially marigolds, the flowers of the dead) and the favourite dishes of the deceased. The offerings can also be taken to the cemetery, but either way, at the end, the prepared dishes are eaten amongst family members and the occasion becomes a merry one. These customs so alien to Europeans have their roots in pre-Columbian traditions.

Voladores

Before the Spanish conquest, the *voladores,* or flying men, plunged from the skies to honour Tonatiuh, the God of the Sun, who year after year brought back spring and fertility to the countryside. Nowadays, the spectacle is performed to earn the pesos of Mexicans and foreigners alike. Where can you admire their flying skills? In Mexico City, in front of the world-famous Museum of Anthropology and at the main archaeological sites. As soon as enough spectators have gathered around the 30-m-high wooden pole, the five splendidly dressed Totonac Indians climb the pole until they reach the top, where they sit on a narrow wooden platform. One of them plays the flute, and soon the other four let themselves fall, their feet held by a rope. In a spiral motion around the pole, they gradually let themselves fall to the ground. Every *volador* circles the pole 13 times, which multiplied by four gives us 52, the pre-Columbian calendar cycle. Once they almost touch the ground, they do a flip, landing on their feet!

The economy

Giant deposits of crude oil were discovered in Mexico in the mid-1970s. In view of this enormous underground wealth, foreign investors generously poured millions into financing the drilling and production facilities. Soon, the country was awash in dollars, and the government as well as the private sector invested heavily: foreign investment doubled, and the national debt climbed to unprecedented levels, soon reaching more than 100 thousand million dollars. When a few years later an oil glut forced prices down, the whole scheme crashed, resulting in incredible losses. Nowadays, Mexico has one of the world's highest debts. Unfortunately, a lot of the loaned money simply disappeared in corrupt pockets, never to be seen again. Mexico is still one of the world's largest crude oil producers, occupying the fifth place in the world.

Since 1988, the free market policies of former president Carlos Salinas de Gortari (who is self-exiled in Dublin) brought some positive changes to the country, unfortunately at the expense of the poor. Salinas sold 1,000

Only for those who don't suffer from vertigo: voladores

inefficient public enterprises, amongst them the main airlines Mexicana and Aeroméxico and almost all banks. With the proceeds from so many sales, part of the national debt was paid off and social programmes financed. Inflation fell from a whopping 159 per cent in 1987 to a manageable 8 per cent seven years later. Nevertheless, by 1997, inflation had started climbing once again (16 per cent) and the national debt reached an astronomical 152 thousand million dollars. The administration of Ernesto Zedillo hopes the tourism industry will bring in much needed hard currency; in 1997 alone, more than nine million tourists visited the country, the great majority from the USA. They leave a total of eight thousand million dollars. The tourism industry already employs 8 per cent of the work force, and it is hoped that international investments in the coming years will result in doubling the industry.

Maize in all its various forms

The wide use of maize in Mexico makes a meal without it almost inconceivable. When on the coast, be sure to sample some of the fresh seafood dishes, too

Food

Moctezuma's gastronomic heritage determines the eating habits of the whole country. Maize (corn) was for the Aztecs and the Maya both food and religion – and in a way that is still the case as Mexicans of all social classes know and love all recipes that contain this wonderful grain.

Breakfast *(desayuno)* is a generous, two-course meal. Included in the *desayuno americano* is a freshly pressed fruit juice or a serving of tropical fruit (generally papaya), followed by eggs, bacon or ham and bread. Mexicans prefer the spicy *huevos rancheros* (fried eggs on tortillas with chilli sauce and refried beans) or *huevos a la mexicana* (scrambled eggs with minced onion, tomatoes and chillies). This is accompanied by a cup of *café americano* (usually rather weak), less often by a *café de olla*, a strong coffee with sugar and cinnamon. In the country where the cocoa bean originated, you should be sure to order a cup of hot chocolate.

Hot food stalls and fruit stands characterize many urban street scenes

After such a good breakfast, it's no wonder that Mexicans eat late: lunch not before 2 pm and supper never earlier than 9 pm. Similar to Mediterranean countries, the biggest meal of the day takes place in the early afternoon, supper is a simple affair.

In coastal regions, a favourite appetizer is *ceviche*, a cocktail made of marinated fish mixed with onion, tomatoes and chillies. Full of vitamins is *guacamole*, made of pureed avocados, lime juice, spices and minced vegetables. It is often served with *tacos*. The indispensable ingredient in the great majority of Mexican dishes is the tortilla in all its endless variations. This ever-present flat cake made from unleavened cornmeal can be fried and rolled, thus becoming a *taco*, most often filled with cheese, chicken or minced meat; when served bathed in a hot red, dark or green sauce, it's an *enchilada*; if it comes to your table covered with sour cream, tomato sauce and grated cheese, then it's called an *enchilada suiza*; the flat, fried tortillas with chicken or meat, refried beans, lettuce, chilli and cheese on top are *tostadas*.

The ever-present ingredients of Mexican cuisine are the hot, spicy sauces

Beans *(frijoles)* accompany almost every dish, often pureed, and are called refried beans *(frijoles refritos)*. More exotic extras are juices from hibiscus flowers or agaves; and braised banana leaves are a speciality in some places.

In some northern restaurants, grilled kid goat *(cabrito)* can be found on the menu. From the western state of Jalisco comes the soup named *pozole*, which is almost a meal in itself, consisting of maize, pork, chillies, onion and many spices. By all means also try the dark sauce called *mole poblano*, a sauce invented in Puebla, which has about two dozen ingredients, amongst them almond paste, chocolate and chillies. Perhaps the most popular fish is *huachinango* (red snapper) and *pescado blanco*, a freshwater fish. Very tasty is fish prepared *a la veracruzana* (Veracruz style), baked in a hot tomato sauce. Season permitting, you can order lobsters, oysters and shrimp. Usually, dessert consists of ice cream *(helado)* or crème caramel *(flan)*.

Drinks

A popular aperitif is piña colada (coconut milk, pineapple juice and rum served with crushed ice) and the world-famous margarita (iced lime juice with a shot of tequila and grenadine, served in a glass with a lick of salt). Mexican beer goes very well with the spicy food. Recommended are Bohemia, Carta Blanca and Corona. Wine production is in its infancy, but you can find a good number of tasty wines much more reasonably priced than the imported ones; also known abroad is the schnapps made from the agave or century plant, the best known being tequila. Whilst young tequila is drunk with salt and lime, aged tequila *(añejo)* is savoured like a good cognac.

Restaurants

Eating in Mexico is an unforgettable experience, a veritable feast for the eyes and the taste buds. A truly Mexican peculiarity are the many fruit stands in the street, where oranges, papayas and pineapples are pressed into juices in front of your eyes. In Mexico City and other colonial cities, historical mansions have been converted into luxurious restaurants. Here, the guests eat in romantic inner courtyards where they can admire the architecture while they listen to the splashing water of the patio fountain and marvel at the tropical vegetation surrounding them. While dining, the guests are often entertained with Mexican folk music. In more modest restaurants, a reasonably priced *comida corrida,* consisting of several small courses, can be had for US $5 to US $8, sometimes including the beverage.

Beach kitchens and restaurants without menus

Even if that fish being grilled in the modest beach kitchen looks so tempting: if there's no menu and the daily fare is communicated to you orally, you should still ask for the price and make sure that both parties have understood and agreed on the terms. This also holds true for drinks. That way, surprises and bad feelings are avoided when the bill arrives at your table.

Montezuma's revenge

A well-known ailment, but the description is not altogether correct. It was Cortés who insisted on writing incorrectly the name of Emperor Montezuma, and everyone copied him. The revenge will sooner or later get almost everybody, from backpackers to those who brush their teeth using mineral water. Granted, there are a few who are immune to it, but successful prevention seems to be the world's best-kept secret. You can reduce your chances of coming down with it by avoiding raw, unwashed vegetables, unpeeled fruit, ice cream of dubious origin, tap water and if you do not accept drinks with ice cubes! If you get it after all, buy the highly effective 'Lomotil', available without prescription from the local pharmacy.

Tequila

Tequila is a small city situated in the state of Jalisco, at the foot of the 3,000-m-high volcano bearing the same name. Surrounding the town are countless plantations of bluish agaves (century plants). It was here, in the 19th century, that someone discovered that a palatable spirit could be obtained by distilling the fermented juice of the heart of the plant. Soon thereafter, row upon row of the agave sprang up across the country, followed by numerous distilleries. But only in Tequila and in Guadalajara are they open to visitors.

Fired, carved and woven handicrafts

From hammocks to wooden figures

The fact that Mexican arts and crafts have their origin in ancient pre-Columbian traditions is a sign of quality. Admittedly, there is kitsch, but it is more the exception than the rule. A wide assortment can be found at the state-owned 'Fonart' shops as well as in the *casas de artesanías*, where you should go first to get an idea what is offered, then go to the markets where prices are flexible and you can haggle. Since there are important regional arts and crafts production centres, you will often find very different articles in different areas.

Some of the best pottery can be admired and purchased in the state of Michoacán. After carefully giving form to the piece, potters put a shiny green coating on it. From the state of Puebla come the impressive trees of life, as well as the beautiful yellow-blue tiles *(azulejos)* decorated with arabesques (introduced after the conquest), as well as the famous blue Talavera china. Near Oaxaca, the characteristic vases

Carpets and other woven articles in Oaxaca are seen in many Indian markets in southern Mexico

are given a shiny, metallic coating (since it contains lead, the Oaxaca pottery should be used only for ornamental purposes). In the potter's town of Tonalá, the ceramics are embellished with colourful, fantastic scenes.

In addition to the large variety of pottery, there are many beautiful and artistic hand-woven textiles of all shapes and sizes, created by the dedicated hands of the Indians, from the traditional wide blouses *(huipiles)* to shawls, skirts, dresses and table cloths. It's better to purchase them directly from Indian women and not in expensive shops, since the craftsmen will receive only a fraction of the price. Delicately painted and varnished wooden boxes and chests of all sizes and shapes come from Uruapan in Michoacán and Olinalá in Guerrero (but they can be bought anywhere); painted wooden animals are made in Oaxaca. The Indians still use and sell their wickerwork for a few pesos. Last but not least, the undisputed symbol of the Mexican 'dolce vita' is the colourful hammock *(hamaca)*, the best selection of which can be found in Mérida (Yucatán).

From the bizarre to the boisterous

*Indian customs, Catholic traditions, patriotic festivities:
in Mexico, there's almost always a fiesta going on*

In Mexico, a celebration takes place every day somewhere, as every town has its own patron saint. City festivals, carnival, Easter and the Day of Independence bring all Mexicans to the streets.

PUBLIC HOLIDAYS

1 January *New Year's Day (Año Nuevo)*

5 February *Day of the Constitution (Aniversario de la Constitución) of 1917*, although the Constitution of 1857 (Benito Juárez) is also honoured

21 March *Birthday of Benito Juárez (Natalicio de B. Juárez)*; patriotic festivities in the schools

1 May *Labour Day (Día del Trabajo)*

5 May *Day of the Battle of Puebla (Aniversario de la Batalla de Puebla)*; victory over the French troops in 1862 is commemorated

1 September *State of the Union Address by the president (Informe Presidencial)*

The multitude of regional festivities bears witness to Mexico's three cultures

16 September ★ *Independence Day (Día de la Independencia)*; the president re-enacts the call for independence of the parish priest Miguel Hidalgo from the balcony of the National Palace *(Grito de Dolores)*

12 October *Columbus Day*, also called *Day of the Race (Día de la Raza)* or *Day of the Americas*; the day when the present Latin American people came into being

20 November *Day of the Revolution (Aniversario de la Revolución) of 1910*

RELIGIOUS HOLIDAYS & FESTIVITIES

Although religious holidays are not official days of rest, they are nevertheless tolerated.

6 January *Epiphany (Los Santos Reyes)*; in Mexico, children receive gifts on this day instead of on Christmas Eve

March/April *Easter week (Semana Santa)* from Thursday to Easter Sunday

1 November ★ *All Souls' Day (Todos los Santos)*

2 November *Day of the Dead (Día de los Muertos)*

27

MARCO POLO SELECTION: EVENTS

1 Grito de Dolores
The call for independence is re-enacted from every balcony in all the city halls of the country (page 27)

2 Voladores in Papantla
This event for tourists becomes a real public festival on Corpus Christi (page 29)

3 Pilgrimage to Guadalupe
All of Central America shows up on 12 December at the church (page 28)

4 Carnival
In every city, but especially in Mérida (page 28)

5 Día de los Muertos
In the night from All Saints' to All Souls' all towns at Lake Pátzcuaro remember their dead (page 27)

6 Patron saint celebrations in Chamula
Nowhere else will you see a more original and unusual festival (page 29)

12 December ★ *Day of the Virgin of Guadalupe (Aparición de la Virgen de Guadalupe)*
25 December *Christmas Day (Navidad)*

FESTIVALS & LOCAL EVENTS

In addition to national celebrations, there are numerous local festivities, which over the years have gained a regional or even national reputation. You can obtain a brochure describing the important festivities and their significance from the tourist information office in Mexico City. A similar, but much more detailed, brochure describing the most important festivities of every state can be obtained from the tourist information office of the corresponding state capital.

In the patron saint festivities honouring the local saint, the high point is a religious procession where the figure of the saint is taken out of the local church and carried through the streets. As the festivities continue into the evening, alcohol and boisterous activity gradually take over.

Patron saint festivities
The festivities honouring the patron saint Prisca of Taxco are held on *18 January*.

City festival
In Guanajuato, from *20 to 22 January*, the whole city celebrates.

Day of San Sebastián
In the town of Chiapa de Corzo (Chiapas), on *20 January*, a mock 'sea battle' is played out on the Río Grijalva.

Carnival
★ A boisterous celebration with colourful floats; one of the best is the carnival of Mérida.

Flower celebration
In the maze formed by the numerous canals of the floating

28

gardens of Xochimilco, south of Mexico City, this famous festival is held on the *Friday before Palm Sunday*.

Dance of the Old Men

The 'Dance of the Frail Men' in Pátzcuaro (Michoacán) and the ★ *voladores celebration* in Papantla (Veracruz) are held on *Corpus Christi*.

Patron saint celebrations

★ In San Juan Chamula (Chiapas) on *24 June*, the local saint is honoured with elaborate equestrian games and processions.

Lunes del Cerro

On top of the Cerro del Fortín in Oaxaca, *during the last two weeks in July*, Indian dances are performed, an event called the 'Guelaguetza'. This celebration takes its origins from a pre-Columbian tradition.

Ascension Day

This important Catholic holiday commemorating the ascent of the Virgin Mary is celebrated nationwide with pilgrimages and dances on *15 August*.

The Santa Rosa festivities

This particularly colourful four-day event starts on *28 August* in San Juan Chamula (Chiapas).

Patron saint festivities

To honour San Miguel, on *29 September*, festivities take place throughout the country, the most elaborate being those of San Miguel de Allende (Guanajuato).

Posadas

From 16 to 24 December, the Holy Family's search for a hostel is re-enacted across the country; groups of children walk from house to house.

The charreadas originated in the northern cattle country

The land of three cultures

Apart from being home to the world's largest metropolis, this region boasts a wealth of monuments from a glorious past: colossal pyramids, magnificent Spanish architecture, VW beetles

Three cultures characterize the landscape in which the world's biggest city is situated. The high volcanoes dominate the horizon. A trip to the central highlands is always a journey to the roots of modern Mexico. The 'Valley of Anáhuac', on a high plateau more than 2,000 m above sea level, is where the first nomadic tribes settled more than 10,000 years ago. Much later, in the 14th century, the Aztecs founded their

The cathedral in Mexico City reaches monumental proportions

capital here. Two centuries later, on the ruins and ashes of the ravaged colossal pyramids and temples, Spanish conquistador Hernán Cortés ordered splendid churches and magnificent palaces to be built. He inaugurated the newly conquered city Ciudad de México, Mexico City, which, today, is the world's most populated metropolis.

In the central highlands, imposing pre-Columbian ruins as well as some of the most beautiful colonial cities await the visitor. In Teotihuacán, the 'Place of the Gods', a mysterious civiliza-

---

Hotel and restaurant prices

Hotels
Category 1: over US $64
Category 2: US $32 to US $64
Category 3: up to US $32
The prices are for one night in a double room, excluding breakfast.

Restaurants
Category 1: over US $19
Category 2: US $6 to US $19
Category 3: under US $6
Prices are for a typical dish from the menu, excluding beverages.

Important abbreviations

Av. Avenida (Avenue)   **Col.** Colonia (district)

tion whose origin is largely unknown built a huge ceremonial centre of epic proportions. In the silver city of Taxco, declared a national monument long ago, silversmiths pursue a tradition that goes back hundreds of years.

This whole region forms part of a massive volcanic chain, the Sierra Volcánica Transversal, which is the country's most important mountain chain and has the highest peaks, some of them snow-capped. Most of the volcanoes are extinct now, but in recent years the Popocatépetl, the most famous and beautiful of all, has once again awakened from its long slumber.

The central highlands make for a very pleasant destination. Thanks to the altitude, the daytime temperatures are mild and spring like. Although sun shines nearly every day, the evenings are usually quite cool.

GUADALAJARA

(165/D3) This busy 5-million metropolis, the country's second largest, unites the advantages and disadvantages of an industrialized city having a rich cultural heritage. From the central *plaza*, it is very easy to reach the imposing palaces and richly adorned churches on foot. In between, there are plenty of cosy cafés where you can relax before continuing. Thanks to intelligent planning in the early 1980s, many streets were converted to pedestrian precincts, thus giving the many *plazas* a romantic and lively atmosphere. In the spring, the lilac blossoms of the massive jacaranda trees bloom everywhere, and the equally large

Indian laurels give plenty of shade to protect the visitor from the hot Mexican sun. Many American tourists like to come in the spring.

SIGHTS

Degollado Theatre
This neoclassical building, whose heavily gilt interior is illuminated by the sparkle of enormous glass chandeliers, is the cultural centre of the city. Get a current programme; many operas, operettas and concerts are performed here. On Sunday mornings, don't miss the show of the 'Grupo Folklórico'. *Mon–Sat 10 am–2 pm, Morelos/Degollado*

Hospicio Cabañas
Inside this enormous former orphanage, built in 1805 and boasting 23 inner courtyards, are the most important works of the famous Mexican painter and muralist José Clemente Orozco, amongst them the world-renowned *Man in Flames*. With fellow artist Diego Rivera, he founded Mexico's contemporary painting school, which blends pre-Columbian elements with the strong colours and heavy brushstrokes of Expressionism. *Tues–Sun 10 am–6 pm, at the end of the Plaza Tapatía, between República and Allende*

Cathedral
The city centre is dominated by the large cathedral, whose construction was started in the 16th century. Over the years, however, many different styles were added, making it an eclectic mix. As the twin spires were destroyed by a powerful earthquake in the early 1900s, they were rebuilt in the Byzantine style. In the sacristy,

MARCO POLO SELECTION: THE CENTRAL HIGHLANDS

1 **Zócalo, Cathedral and National Palace**
A trio of superlatives in the centre of Mexico City (pages 41–42)

2 **Casa de los Azulejos**
Restaurant and shop in a beautiful, historical building (page 44)

3 **Teotihuacán**
A 2,000-year-old 'City of the Gods' (page 47)

4 **Guanajuato**
Picturesque mining town full of romantic cobbled streets (page 37)

5 **Taxco**
Hills, silver and charming cobbled streets (page 61)

6 **Santa María de Tonantzintla**
The small church is the high point of Mexican Baroque (page 55)

you can admire a masterpiece by the famous Spanish painter Bartolomé Esteban Murillo (*The Assumption*). *Alcalde/Hidalgo*

Palacio de Gobierno
This building, built in 1643, has been silent witness to many im-

Six architectural styles combine to form Guadalajara's cathedral

portant historical moments. In 1858, for example, President Benito Juárez found refuge here from his political persecutors. On the wall beside the flight of stairs leading to the upper floor of this Baroque palace, you can admire a monumental *mural* painted by Orozco, showing the valiant struggle of Father Hidalgo for freedom against the army and the church. *Morelos/Pino Suárez (Plaza de Armas)*

Plazas
The cathedral is surrounded by four beautiful *plazas*. On the portal side is the ✝ *Plaza de los Laureles*, the plaza of the Indian laurel trees. The dense crowns of the deep green trees provide welcome shade for the many young people who congregate here. Between the cathedral and the Palacio de Gobierno lies the *Plaza de Armas* with the well-known Victorian circular stage. On the other side of the church, one runs into the

Rotonda de los Hombres Ilustres, a well-kept park with life-size bronze statues of past patriots. Last but not least, behind the cathedral, you will find the *Plaza de la Liberación* with colonial fountains and a statue of Hidalgo. This *plaza* is also called Plaza de los Tres Poderes because the city hall, the legislative building and the palace of justice surround it.

Plaza Tapatía
At the end of the long pedestrian precinct from the cathedral to the Hospicio Cabañas is the Plaza Tapatía with an attractive fountain, many statues and many businesses housed in modern buildings.

Church of Santa Mónica
The façade of this Augustinian church built in 1718 is widely regarded as a Baroque jewel owing to its exquisite stone masonry. *Santa Mónica, between Reforma and San Felipe*

Museo Regional
In a building dating back to the 18th century, and in many rooms separated by patios, many works of art from pre-Columbian times to the 19th century are exhibited. Especially interesting are the carriages of the two rivals, Emperor Maximilian and President Juárez. *Tues–Sun 9 am – 4 pm, Hidalgo/Liceo at the Plaza de la Liberación*

La Casa de los Mariscos
The name says it all: fish and shellfish prepared the Jalisco way. *Morelos 1443/Colonias, Tel. 013/ 826 17 57, category 2*

La Estancia Gaucha
❖ Popular amongst the locals; the speciality: Argentinian steaks and seafood. *Niños Héroes 2860-A, Tel. 013/122 65 65, category 2*

Fridas
A cosy cafeteria that also serves breakfast; decorated with tiles by Jorge Wilmot. *Marcos Castellanos/ López Cotilla (at the Parque de la Revolución), Tel. 013/826 17 87, category 2*

Sanborns
This chain of restaurants and crafts shops has several outlets in Guadalajara. Recommended for a snack (soup, salad, sandwiches) and for Mexican dishes. *López Mateos Sur 2718, Tel. 013/ 647 52 54, category 2–3*

La Troje
Mexican cuisine with a varied folklore show: *mariachis*, folkloric dances, performers (daily from 4 pm). *Av. Américas 1311, Tel. 013/817 17 17, category 2*

El Charro
Those who would like to dress up like a Mexican cowboy (*charro*) will find all they need. The complete *charrería* wardrobe is here: all the way from sombreros, leather belts, riding whips and jackets to saddle bags, embroidered shirts and gloves. *Juárez 148*

Mercado Libertad
❖ The city's biggest market is housed in a modern and rather unattractive building and caters mostly to the locals, but is nevertheless an interesting place for the visitor because of the con-

stant activity and the many gourmet stands. On the upper floor, small modest restaurants serve all imaginable Mexican dishes. *Javier Mina/Cabañas*

ACCOMMODATION

Carlton Hotel
The former Sheraton is the only luxury hotel in the city centre. *250 rooms, Av. Niños Héroes/16 de Septiembre, Tel. 013/614 72 72, Fax 613 55 39, category 1*

Francés
This old city palace was built in 1610 and is now a national monument. Beautifully restored; full of colonial charm. *60 rooms, Av. Maestranza 35, Tel. 013/613 11 90, Fax 658 28 31, category 2*

Hamilton
Economical rooms and centrally located. *32 rooms, Madero 381 (between Galeana and Ocampo), Tel. 013/614 67 26, Fax 658 19 25, category 3*

ENTERTAINMENT

Gourmet Jazz
♯ Popular jazz melodies attract the crowds. *Marcos Castellanos/López Cotilla*

La Rondella
♩♪ The view from the cabaret located in the 20th storey of the Carlton Hotel is unforgettable. *Mon–Sat 9 pm–2 am, Av. Niños Héroes/16 de Septiembre*

Salón Veracruz
✪ A place where couples can dance until the early morning hours. Good salsa rhythms. *Manzano 486 (beside the Carlton Hotel)*

INFORMATION

Mexicana
Mariano Otero 2353, Tel. 013/112 00 11

Tourist information
Morelos 102 (Plaza Tapatía), Tel. 013/614 01 23, Fax 613 11 85, www.Jalisco.gob.mx

SURROUNDING AREA

There are many destinations near Guadalajara that will give you a glimpse of the more peaceful, provincial Jalisco. Rustic villages, colonial cities and pretty landscapes are all within easy reach.

Lake Chapala   (165/D3-4)
The Lago de Chapala, situated about 60 km south-east of Guadalajara, is Mexico's largest natural lake, but it is rapidly shrinking as can be seen in its eastern and southern shorelines. The pleasant climate and the varied landscape have made the northern shoreline a preferred second home of many retired Americans (especially Ajijic).
   The three villages on the northern shoreline are ideal for strolls: *Chapala* lures with a Mexican-American flair and houses built in pseudo-Victorian style surrounded by colourful bougainvilleas and one of the most beautiful hotels, the *Quinta Quetzalcóatl*, a restored manor house *(8 suites, Zaragoza 307, Tel. 01376/536 53, Fax 534 44, category 1)*. This is the place where, in 1923, D.H. Lawrence wrote his famous novel about Mexico, *The Plumed Serpent* (1926), whose main theme is the

clash between Indian and Western world views.

Ajijic, on the other hand, is one of Jalisco's most beautiful colonial towns. From the central *plaza*, you can see a wide selection of boutiques selling elegant embroidered blouses, crafts shops and galleries, many located in former Spanish manor houses.

Neighbouring *Jocotepec* was founded back in 1528 and every Thursday is *tianguis* — market day — when the Indians, descendants of the Nahuas (Aztecs) who settled around the lake long before the Spaniards, come down to sell their woven articles, such as bright ponchos, blankets and carpets.

Those who would like to stay longer can rent a holiday flat. The selection of affordable accommodation is large.

Tequila (164/D3)

Large fields of agaves (century plants) characterize the landscape of Jalisco. An astounding 70 million litres of the clear, potent schnapps are distilled every year at this Mexican plant. This small city, 60 km north-west of Guadalajara, gave the spirit its name. Nowadays, many distilleries open their doors to visitors and demonstrate the distillation process. At the end of the tour, the visitor is allowed to taste the source of the city's wealth.

Tlaquepaque (165/D3)

The main attraction of this town, located only 7 km away from Guadalajara, is its countless arts and crafts shops and workshops. The former village of glass-blowers slowly metamorphosed into the preferred shopping destination for all kinds of Mexican products. The selection is huge: antique furniture can be found, for example, at the *Antigua de México (Independencia 255,* shipping can be arranged). In the gallery of *Sergio Bustamante (Independencia 238)*, the artist himself sells his world-renowned sculptures made of papier mâché and copper. In attractive cafés, you can rest from all the shopping while the *mariachis* play a tune. A good selection of healthy dishes with delicious drinks (Friday and Saturday accompanied by live music) and unique décor characterize *Casa Vieja (Guillermo Prieto 99/Constitución, Tel. 013/ 657 62 50, category 2)*.

Tonalá (165/D3)

A well-known potter's town 12 km south of Guadalajara on the road to the airport and Lake Chapala, Tonalá has been able to retain its rustic, peaceful atmosphere much more than its counterpart, Tlaquepaque, although the metropolis comes closer every day. Dozens of workshops and businesses lure passersby to browse. Apart from offering kitchenware, the town is known for its animal figures. On Sundays and Thursdays (market days), the many beautiful ceramics are put on display outside, along the streets and in the squares. In *Calle Hidalgo*, you can find the workshop of *José Bernabé Campechano*, who with the help of his seven sons produces the *petatillos*, the most beautiful hand-painted decorative plates.

GUANAJUATO

(166/A3) ★ Known throughout the world, Guanajuato is one of the most beautiful colonial cities in Mexico. Situated in a narrow valley at an altitude of 2,000 m, this college town and state capital of 130,000 souls has a lively atmosphere thanks to the many *plazas*, a maze of narrow cobbled streets, steep walkways and colourful façades. Many streets are underground, built on the dry riverbed or former mining shafts, giving the city a most original aspect. As it's easy to get lost, it's advisable to take a taxi from the outskirts to the central square and to explore the romantic-gloomy streets from there.

The air improves as you leave the narrow streets along *El Subterráneo* and approach *El Callejón del Beso*. In the 'Narrow Street of the Kiss', it would have been possible for Romeo to kiss Juliet from his balcony, so close are the balconies to each other! Greatly contributing to the atmosphere is the music played and heard in this charming city. For example, in the central square pavilion, the *Jardín de la Unión*, an orchestra plays; the colonial tradition of the *estudiantinas*

Guanajuato's colourful, narrow streets

(strolling student bands that walk and play through the narrow streets after dusk) is very much alive. As they sing and play the guitar, they pull the people behind them.

The city is a veritable treasure trove of wonderful colonial buildings, a vestige of colonial wealth: the Spaniards discovered several large silver mines here. In the squares, it's still possible to see the ancient mining wagons, now filled with plants.

SIGHTS

Alhóndiga de Granaditas

✦ Called 'Mexico's Bastille' by some, this fortress-like corn silo of huge proportions played an important role in the bloody War of Independence. José Martínez, a young Indian miner, risking his own life, managed to blow up the massive entrance to the silo where the royalist troops had retreated, allowing the rebels to enter the building and claim the city. It was only a temporary victory for Father Hidalgo; later, the Spaniards captured and executed the leaders. For several years, people could see their heads being displayed in the four corners of the Alhóndiga. Nowadays, the building is a national memorial and houses a *regional museum* exhibiting documents relating to the War of Independence and to the extraction of silver. *Tues–Sat 10 am–2 pm and 4 pm–6 pm, Sun 10 am–3 pm, 28 de Septiembre/Mendizábal*

Jardín de la Unión

Street life takes place under the cool shade of the massive Indian laurels. Diners can be seen in the surrounding restaurants until late at night. The Posada

Santa Fé, a hotel since 1862, is worth a visit.

El Pípila
The best panoramic view of the city is from the large memorial that the city fathers built in honour of José Martínez, called El Pípila. It is best to take a taxi in the late afternoon (best light for photos) to the memorial, enjoy the view from above and then stroll down to the city centre. *Carretera Panorámica, south-east of the city*

Plaza de la Paz
Once the favourite address of the silver barons, whose palaces frame the small square, the best of all is the former residence of Count Rul y Valenciana, owner of the silver mine bearing his name. The magnificent palace, where the famous German naturalist and explorer Alexander von Humboldt once spent the night, was renovated in the 18th century by the famous Mexican architect Eduardo Tresguerras. *Av. Juárez, west of the Jardín de la Unión*

Teatro Benito Juárez
In this splendid neoclassical building, finished in 1903, the centre of the yearly Cervantes festival, the country's most important cultural event, Yehudi Menuhin has already played. The interior must be seen: Doric columns support the roof, from which the nine muses look down to the plush, gold and stucco. *Tues–Sun 9 am–2 pm and 5 pm–7 pm, Sopeña, southern end of the Jardín de la Unión*

Universidad
The conspicuous university building is reached by a massive stairway. It was built in 1955 on the spot of a former Jesuit school in a Moorish style. The view from the building of the old town is very good. Beside it is the *Compañía Church* (1765). *Positos*

MUSEUMS

Museo Casa Diego Rivera
The place of pilgrimage for art-lovers is the house where the great muralist was born. It is built in colonial Guanajuato style and the interior houses approximately one hundred of his works. *Daily 10 am–1 pm and 4 pm–6 pm, Positos 47*

Museo Iconográfico de Quijote
Guanajuato honours the great Miguel de Cervantes like no other city in the world. Every year, the Cervantes Festival takes place here, a three-week event in October when the 'Entremeses Cervantinos', one-act plays written by Cervantes himself, are enacted. Jazz and classical music concerts are also held. In a beautifully restored colonial building, now converted into a museum, pictures and precious first editions of *Don Quixote*, the 'Knight of the Sad Countenance', can be admired. Former Spanish Prime Minister Felipe González, present at the inauguration, regretted that his homeland had nothing comparable to offer. The exhibition pieces, some even 300 years old, were a gift from Eulalio Ferrer, a Spanish exile living in Mexico since 1941 who made a fortune in advertising. *Tues–Sat 10 am–6 pm, Sun 10 am–3 pm, Manuel Doblado 1*

Museo de las Momias
Mexicans have a relaxed attitude towards death. On the way to the city cemetery, there is a

unique museum: behind glass, in a vacuum, there are 119 mummies, most of them standing and assembled in groups, facing the visitors. Some of them even have shreds of their clothes hanging from their bodies! A sight definitely not for the squeamish! Most of them are about one hundred years old, some merely a few decades, and in every case they are exhibited with the family's permission. Supposedly, the particular geologic conditions of Guanajuato, namely the mineral-rich soil and the bone-dry air, accelerate the perfect mummification of the corpses. Mexican families think highly of the gruesome exhibit, foreigners are taken aback! *Daily, 9 am–6 pm, Cementerio Municipal, Explanada de Panteón, Tepetapa, north-west of the centre*

RESTAURANTS

Breakfast cafés and open-air restaurants full of atmosphere border the Jardín de la Unión.

Casa Valadez
Mexican cuisine served in the open air at the central square. *Jardín de la Unión 3, Tel. 01473/211 57, category 2*

Mariscos El Callejón
Centrally located in the busy main street, the specialities are shellfish and fish dishes. *Av. Juárez 192, Tel. 01473/227 89, category 2*

Posada Santa Fé
The impressive dining room of this hotel-restaurant resembles a museum. Mexican cuisine amid a relaxed atmosphere. *Jardín de la Unión 12, Tel. 01473/200 84, category 2*

El Patio
A patio-restaurant serving all the tasty Mexican delicacies, from guacamole to tamales. *Av. Juárez 226, Tel. 01473/222 94, category 2*

SHOPPING

In Guanajuato, you can purchase inexpensive watercolours and oils depicting the picturesque buildings of the city; they are often seen in squares and along the streets. Worth a visit is the *Mercado Hidalgo (Av. Juárez)* housed in a metallic Art Nouveau structure.

ACCOMMODATION

Hostería del Frayle
This four-storeyed hotel was originally the city's mint and dates back to the 17th century. *37 rooms, Sopeña 3, Tel. 01473/201 88, Fax 211 79, category 2*

Parador San Javier
Stylish luxury in a former hacienda of the 17th century with its own chapel. Quiet location only 2 km away from the city centre. *112 rooms, Plaza Aldama 92, Tel. 01473/206 50, Fax 231 14, category 1*

Posada Santa Fé
This old inn has offered sleeping accommodation since 1862. A café on the ground floor has been the traditional meeting place of artists and intellectuals for decades. *48 rooms, Jardín de la Unión 12, Tel. 01473/200 84, Fax 246 53, category 2*

INFORMATION

Tourist information
Plaza de la Paz 14, Tel. 01473/219 82, Fax 242 51, www.int.com.mx/guanajuato

MEXICO CITY

☛ City Map inside back cover

(166/C4-5) The monstrous immensity of Mexico City (Ciudad de México) can best be appreciated from the airplane, an endless maze of streets and flat roofs, skyscrapers and a few parks stretching into the horizon. As the airplane is about to land, you can discern the domes of churches, colonial palaces, wide avenues and huge monuments. If the weather is clear, towards the east, you'll have an impressive view of the two snow-capped volcanoes, Popocatépetl and Ixtaccíhuatl. Sadly, the two gigantic landmarks are seen only rarely once you are in the usually smoggy city down below. More than three million vehicles and approximately 100,000 factories contaminate the air, and one-third of the population still cooks with charcoal. It strains the imagination that 100 years ago, this 2,000-m-high city had air so clear that it was considered a health resort, where tuberculosis patients from the humid lowlands were taken. To solve the severe air pollution problem, the production of 30,000 electric automobiles has begun. Most of them will be used as taxis, eventually replacing the ubiquitous VW beetles, the rest will be exported to the USA and Canada.

The Paseo de la Reforma, an impressive and, in some places, ten-lane wide boulevard forms the central axis of the metropolis, together with the 40-km-long Avenida Insurgentes. Day after day, the 25 million inhabitants of metropolitan Mexico City crowd the underground, buses and streets. Tens of thousands of honking, polluting automobiles inch their way through the clogged streets, and only until late in the evening is the city quiet once again. The few green lungs of the city are Alameda Park and the much bigger Chapultepec Park, where on weekends working-class families love to picnic while watching the clowns and travelling entertainers.

Greatness and poverty, splendour and squalor, are constantly seen side by side. The fashionable Zona Rosa, the shopping and entertainment centre, is the preferred meeting place of the rich and famous. Well-dressed businessmen easily spend in one meal what a maid earns in one month, while shoe-cleaners offer their services outside and Indian women carrying their youngest baby are hypnotized by the elegant shop windows displaying the latest fashions.

The most important colonial buildings cluster around the Zócalo, the huge square at the city centre, on which nowadays festivities and parades take place. Inside the beautiful National Palace, seat of the executive offices, one of Diego Rivera's most famous murals, the historical *Epic of the Mexican People*, vividly portrays the high points of the country's bloody history.

Mexico City rests on historical soil: where the old, heavy colonial buildings now stand, even older Aztec pyramids, temples and palaces once stood. When the Aztecs arrived in the early 14th century and saw an eagle perched on a cactus, devouring a snake, they recognized the prophesied sign they had been waiting for and founded Tenochtitlán in 1325. The bellicose Aztecs soon conquered the earlier

The Floating Gardens of Xochimilco: a popular weekend destination

settlers, founding a mighty empire, only to see it crumble to dust two centuries later, victims of the conquistadors and the smallpox they brought with them. The Spaniards lost no time destroying the fragile ecosystem by drying up the lakes and felling all trees. The still existing 'Floating Gardens' of Xochimilco, a maze of canals in the southern part of the city, are the only reminder of what was once a beautiful pre-Columbian metropolis.

SIGHTS

Basílica de Guadalupe (O)
❂ On 9 December 1531, according to legend, the Indian Juan Diego saw a vision of a dark-skinned Virgin Mary urging him to see the bishop so that a church in her honour would be built. As proof, she gave the young man an enormous rose bouquet (roses didn't grow on the dry hill), which he took in his folded cloak. When the Indian opened his cloak upon seeing the bishop, a beautiful image of the Virgin was seen imprinted on the cloth. The church

to honour 'La Morena', the dark-skinned one, was soon built, and it quickly became the most important place of pilgrimage. Every 12th day of December, millions pour into this holy place to see the imprinted cloth showing Mexico's patron saint. The Virgin is now housed in a large, modern basilica and the image is encased in glass high above the altar, enabling everybody to see her. *Calzada Guadalupe, Metro: Basílica*

Catedral Metropolitana (U/F3)
★ The dimensions of this cathedral, the largest on the continent, are truly colossal. Take your time to admire the exquisite work of the stonemasons around the *portals*, and inside the masterpiece of Jerónimo de Balbás, the ornately decorated *Altar of the Kings* (Altar de los Reyes) and the fantastic *choir stalls* carved from cedar by Juan de Rojas. Don't be surprised by all the scaffolds inside. They serve the function of supporting the sinking 3,000-tonne-structure. *Daily, 8 am–6 pm, northern side of the Zócalo, Metro: Zócalo*

Chapultepec Park (U/A4-5)

This huge park is the local equivalent of Hyde Park or Central Park, and it offers everything: secluded groves, vast meadows, lakes, even a zoo. On top of a steep hill lies *Chapultepec Castle*, now a museum, which was the former residence of Emperor Maximilian. Built in the 18th century on 'Grasshopper Hill', it was first used as barracks, then as a military academy. The *Monument to the Heroic Children* (Monumento a los Niños Héroes) at the entrance to the park commemorates the young cadets who lost their lives during the Mexican-American War in 1846–48. *Reforma/ Melchor Ocampo, Metro: Chapultepec*

Palacio Nacional (U/F3)

★ The National Palace, once the palace of Hernán Cortés, is the city's largest secular colonial building. It has been restored and rebuilt several times since the first stone was laid. The part open to the public displays the colourful historical *murales* by Diego Rivera on the walls of the upper floor, which depict scenes of everyday life of several Indian cultures before the conquest, a magnet for tourists, teachers and school children. *Tues–Sun 9 am–6 pm, eastern side of the Zócalo, Metro: Zócalo*

Plaza de las Tres Culturas (O)

On the historical Plaza of the Three Cultures, a plaque by the ruins of pre-Columbian temples reminds visitors that on 13 August 1521, after a long siege, the proud Indian capital fell into the hands of Hernán Cortés: 'It was neither a triumph nor a defeat, but the painful birth of Mexico and the mestizo people.' The small church of Santiago Tlatelolco, built in 1609, represents the colonial era, while modern skyscrapers symbolize modern Mexico, amongst them the Foreign Ministry. *Metro: Tlatelolco*

Templo Mayor (U/F3)

In a letter to Charles V, Cortés mentioned that the Aztec temple was 'taller than the Cathedral of Seville'. Nowadays, archaeologists have uncovered the impressive foundation walls. Elevated footbridges (the former temple has also sunk several metres owing to the city's sinking aquifers) afford a good view of both modern and Spanish colonial buildings on the Zócalo. *Tues–Sun 9 am–5 pm, north-east of the Zócalo, Metro: Zócalo*

Torre Latinoamericana (U/E3)

While you enjoy your meal or cocktail from the restaurant located on the 42nd floor, you can take in the fantastic view from above. The architect of the 177-m-high structure is proud that his skyscraper has withstood all earthquakes without having been damaged. *Daily, 10 am–11 pm, Madero/ Lázaro Cárdenas, Metro: Bellas Artes, admission US $2.50*

Zócalo (U/F3)

★ Every year, in the night from 15 to 16 September, the huge, empty Zócalo fills with up to a million people waiting to hear the re-enact-ment of Hidalgo's cry for Independence. Each side of the giant square measures 240 m, making it the world's second largest and the oldest on the continent. The Zócalo 'was levelled, consumed by fires, flooded. It was the scene of excited demonstrations…', writes

Zócalo

This huge square between the cathedral and the National Palace in Mexico City was laid out by Hernán Cortés himself. It was empty for a long time until it was decided to place a statue in the middle. The base *(zócalo)* was completed first, then the statue of the Spanish king was placed there. Until the early 1950s, the central square had fountains, greenery and benches, which were later torn down (there are plans to beautify it once again). It serves as a good meeting place, especially under the gigantic flag. The name 'zócalo' stuck, and since then in almost every major Mexican city, the central square is referred to as such.

the world-renowned writer and diplomat Carlos Fuentes about this most important spot in the history of the world, once the heart of the mighty Aztec Empire, then the colonial capital of New Spain, whose buildings were built by the wealth that silver brought, then becoming the Plaza de la Constitución, or Constitution Square, symbol of independent Mexico. At exactly 6 pm every day, the huge Mexican flag, the country's largest, is taken down by the national guard that emerges from the National Palace. *Metro: Zócalo*

MUSEUMS

Museo Nacional de Antropología (U/A4)

Before the entrance to this giant museum, an 8-m-high, carved monolith representing Tláloc, the rain god, can be admired. This museum is one of the world's best. On the ground floor, the archaeological exhibits are distributed throughout 12 halls. Whereas the first three give an introduction to archaeology, the others are devoted to pre-Columbian civilizations. The upper floor contains objects pertaining to the ethnology of the Indian communities.

Although you should take your time, be sure not to miss the museum's unquestionable magnet: the world-famous Aztec Calendar Stone in Hall 7 (diameter: 3.6 m), a truly impressive representation of the sun god Tonatiuh and the Aztec universe. *Tues–Sat 9 am–7 pm, Sun 10 am–6 pm, Paseo de la Reforma/Calzada Gandhi, Metro: Chapultepec*

Museo Franz Mayer (U/E3)

In the large rooms of this former Augustinian monastery of the 16th century, a fascinating private collection of Mexican and European works of art from the 16th to 20th century are tastefully exhibited. Some of the finest antique furniture and ancient Indian textiles can be admired here. The impressive private library of this reclusive German immigrant and eclectic art collector, who passed away in 1975, can also be visited. *Tues–Sun 10 am–5 pm, Av. Hidalgo 45, Metro: Bellas Artes*

Museo Frida Kahlo (O)

The former home of this increasingly famous painter has been converted into a museum. Kahlo lived here with her husband, Diego Rivera, from 1929 until her death in 1954. *Tues–Sun 10 am–2 pm and 3 pm–6 pm, Londres 247/Allende, Metro: Coyoacán*

Papalote – Museo del Niño   (O)

A lot of fun and yet educational, this 'Children's Museum' offers a unique introduction to natural science in a playful and interactive way. It's fun for parents, too. *Mon–Fri 9 am–1 pm and 2 pm–6 pm, Sat/Sun 10 am–2 pm and 3 pm–7 pm, Av. Constituyentes 268, no close underground station, www.papalote.org.mx*

RESTAURANTS

Casa de los Azulejos (Sanborns)   (U/E3)

★ This restaurant occupies a closed inner courtyard at the centre of a mansion dating from 1750, whose façade is covered by stucco and the typical blue-and-white tiles from Puebla. Good selection of Mexican dishes. *Av. Madero 4, Metro: Bellas Artes, Tel. 015/510 96 13, category 3*

Casa de los Cántaros   (O)

Not only are the Mexican recipes inspired by Frida Kahlo, but the interior decoration as well, with blue-yellow tiles and many arts and crafts. *Plateros 27 (Insurgentes Sur), Col. San José Insurgentes, Metro: Coyoacán, Tel. 015/598 89 90, category 1–2*

Isadora   (O)

The restaurant Isadora may be counted amongst a select number of 'in' places. Hostess Carmen Ortuño puts her latest Mexican culinary creations on the table. *Molière 50, Metro: Polanco, Tel. 015/280 55 86, category 1*

Majestic Hotel (rooftop terrace)   (U/F3)

People come here less for the food than for the view: from this large terrace, decorated with flowers, you get a wonderful view of the Zócalo; in the evening, it is especially romantic, when all the colonial buildings are lit up. Mexican buffet on Sundays. *Madero 73, Metro: Zócalo, Tel. 015/521 86 00, category 2*

Bar Opera   (U/E3)

Pancho Villa once dined here, leaving a hole in the ceiling from his revolver as proof of his visit during the Mexican Revolution. The wainscotted interior and the good food are enticing, even for afternoon tea. *5 de Mayo 10, Metro: Bellas Artes, Tel. 015/512 89 59, category 2*

Café de Tacuba   (U/E3)

This beautiful restaurant, which opened in 1912, is decorated with painted tiles and Belle Epoque furnishings. The specialities are *enchiladas, carne asada* and *chiles rellenos.* The café is a favourite meeting place amongst locals for breakfast. *Tacuba 28, Metro: Bellas Artes, Tel. 015/518 49 50, category 2*

SHOPPING

As would be expected, in Mexico's largest city, the selection of arts and crafts is particularly good. The Pink Zone has many exclusive boutiques, but expect to pay high prices (Zona Rosa, between *Av. Insurgentes, Av. Chapultepec* and *Paseo de la Reforma*).

Bazar Sábado   (O)

The bazaar is held every Saturday in the attractive district of San

Ángel. One of the best selections of paintings and handicrafts can be found at the *Plaza San Jacinto (no underground).*

Buenavista (U/D2)
A huge arts-and-crafts store close to the Buenavista railway station. *Daily 9 am–6 pm, Aldama 187, Col. Guerrero, Metro: Guerrero*

Fonart
A good government-owned 'Fonart' shop with a fine selection and fixed prices is located in Alemada Park. The salespeople are knowledgeable. *Av. Juárez 89 (**U/E3**, Metro: Bellas Artes)* also in *Londres 136 (**U/C4**, Metro: Insurgentes)*

Galería Reforma (U/E3)
A huge market offering leather goods, jewellery, ceramics and wickerwork. Not far from Alameda Park. *Paseo de la Reforma Norte, Metro: Hidalgo*

Sanborns (U/E3)
In this 'Sanborns', you will find an excellent selection of all kinds of Mexican craft in four rooms of the upper floor. Outstanding selection of lacquerwork. The restaurant in the inner courtyard is described on p. 44. *Casa de los Azulejos, Av. Madero 4, Metro: Bellas Artes*

is described on p. 44.

ACCOMMODATION

Del Ángel (U/C4)
Modern hotel in the Zona Rosa. *102 rooms, Río Lerma 154, Metro: Insurgentes, Tel. 015/533 10 32, Fax 533 10 27, category 2*

Camino Real (U/A3)
Luxurious hotel in quiet surroundings near Chapultepec Park. *706 rooms, Mariano Escobedo 700, Metro: Auditorio, Tel. 015/203 21 21, Fax 250 68 97, category 1, www.caminoreal.com/mexico*

El Salvador (U/F4)
☂ The outside is not very attractive, but the rooms are quite nice. Near the Zócalo. *52 rooms, República de El Salvador 16, Metro: Zócalo, Tel. 015/521 10 08, Fax 521 12 47, category 3*

Getting around in Mexico City

As a tourist, you can feel fairly safe throughout Mexico – but that doesn't apply to the capital. Therefore, as an extra precaution, leave your passport, airplane ticket and money in the hotel safe, taking only what you really need. Be sure to make a note of the telephone number to call if your credit card is stolen, put your pocketbook in your front pocket and hold on to your bag tightly. Don't walk too close to the street and where there are too many people, such as in markets, bus and train stations, watch out for pickpockets! During peak hours (in the mornings until 10 am, afternoons from 4 pm to 7 pm), avoid riding the underground. In some stations, men and women must ride separately. The masses trying to get into the carriages can crush the unwary visitor – and even if you manage to get inside, it's certainly not a pleasant experience!

Gran Hotel (U/F3)

The Belle Epoque furnishings of the lobby have already served as a backdrop for a film. *125 rooms, 16 de Septiembre 82, Metro: Zócalo, Tel. 015/510 40 40, Fax 512 67 72, category 1*

Majestic (U/F3)

〰️ A colonial hotel rich in tradition. Good view of the Zócalo from the bar and the rooftop restaurant. *85 rooms, Av. Madero 73, Metro: Zócalo, Tel. 015/521 86 00, Fax 512 62 62, category 2*

Patria (U/F4)

A modest hotel, ideally located in the city centre. *51 rooms, República de El Salvador 137, Metro: Zócalo, Tel. 015/522 40 80, Fax 522 39 47, category 3*

ENTERTAINMENT

Hotel de Cortés (U/E3)

The crowds are large when the *fiestas mexicanas* are held every Saturday: delicious Mexican dishes, mixed drinks and performances by folklore dancers and singers. *Av. Hidalgo 85, Metro: Hidalgo*

Jorongo Bar (U/C4)

In the tastefully decorated bar of the elegant María Isabel Sheraton, some of the best *mariachi* music can be heard. *Reforma 325, Metro: Insurgentes*

Palacio de Bellas Artes (U/E3)

The palace of Fine Arts is an enormous building, a combination of Art Nouveau and Art Déco, featuring huge *murales* by the country's most celebrated painters. The performances of the 'Ballet Folklórico' are especially recommended, but be sure to purchase the tickets in advance. *Lázaro Cárdenas/5 de Mayo, Metro: Bellas Artes, Tel. 015/512 36 33, performances Sun and Wed, www.cia-teq.mx/intelnet/ballet*

El Patio (U/D3-4)

This has been one of the most popular night clubs for years. *Thurs–Sat 9 am–4 am, Atenas 9, Metro: Cuauhtémoc*

Plaza Garibaldi (U/E3)

🎋 A must: soon after dusk, this *plaza* north of Bellas Artes is at its busiest, when *mariachi* bands offer their varied repertoire for a price. *Lázaro Cárdenas/Honduras, Metro: Garibaldi*

INFORMATION

Tourist information (O)

Amberes 54/Londres, Metro: Insurgentes, Tel. 015/525 93 80, Fax 525 93 88

SURROUNDING AREA

Cuernavaca (166/C5)

This city has long been an oasis for the inhabitants of Mexico City. It's only 75 km south of the capital and is easily reached by a modern highway. The eternally mild climate and the tropical colours of the fuchsia bougainvillea, lavender-blue jacarandas and bright orange-red blossoms of the flame trees growing in every garden characterize this city of 800,000 inhabitants. Back in the 1930s, Canadian Malcolm Lowry found in Cuernavaca the inspiration he needed for his masterpiece *Under the Volcano* (1947), a novel that described the last drunken day in the life of the former British consul. The cultural icon of the city is the large *Palacio de Cortés* (1529) in the main square and with a wonderful mural by Diego Rivera, who was commissioned to paint it by Dwight Morrow, the American ambassador at the time and an ardent fan of both Rivera and Cuernavaca (Morrow's daughter married Charles Lindbergh shortly thereafter). The mural colourfully chronicles Morelos history, from the Spanish conquest to Emiliano Zapata. Look out for the portrait of Morelos, which, in fact, is a self-portrait of the artist. The premier culinary destination is the legendary *Las Mañanitas*, located in a large, enchanting tropical garden, with a small *hotel (22 rooms)*; peacocks, macaws, toucans and cranes strut past dining VIPs. *(R. Linares 107, Tel. 0173/14 14 66, Fax 18 36 72, category 1).*

Popocatépetl (166/C5)

Popocatépetl (5,452 m) is not the country's highest mountain as many believe, but certainly the most famous. It lies only 85 km south-east of the capital. It used to be a popular destination for hikers and nature-lovers, but the dormant volcano started showing signs of volcanic activity in 1996, whereupon access to it was promptly prohibited. The name comes from the Aztec, meaning 'smoking mountain', an appropriate name. The sister volcano, Ixtaccíhuatl, has long been extinct (the name means 'sleeping woman' — a name given to the giant volcano because it resembles a woman lying on her back). In 1519, the conquistadors reached the Aztec capital by walking between the two volcanoes. Eyewitness accounts report that the 'Popo' (as it is affectionately called) was active at the time, so Cortés sent some of his men to the rim of the crater to collect sulphur for making gun powder. Ever since the conquest, the high mountain pass has been called *El Paso de Cortés.*

Teotihuacán (166/C4)

★ 'They called the place Teotihuacán, because this is where they buried their kings', wrote the Franciscan monk and scholar Bernardino de Sahagún (1499–1570) in one of the first books written about Mexico. Sadly, we know next to nothing about the continent's most impressive archaeological site,

The mighty Sun Pyramid was built without the aid of draught animals or the wheel

named by the UNESCO a World Cultural Heritage Site. The site is so large and fascinating that you should plan at least half a day for it, preferably in the morning. The pyramids are easily reached from Mexico City, as they are only 50 km north-east of it.

Once you have passed through the main gate, you'll see a pyramid group called The Citadel. Especially noteworthy is the beautifully carved façade of the Quetzalcoátl temple, which depicts the rain god Tláloc and the plumed serpent. Why the Teotihuacans built another pyramid on top of this one (a common practice) will forever remain a mystery. From there, the 40-m-wide Causeway of the Dead *(Camino de los Muertos)* leads directly to the colossal 🐌 *Pyramid of the Sun,* a truly impressive, 63-m-high structure, almost as wide as the Cheops Pyramid of Egypt, but built without the help of the wheel or draught animals. It is believed that construction lasted about 20 years for builders to move 2.5 million tonnes of earth and stone, day and night without interruption. The pyramid was built around the year 100, about 500 years after the place had been settled (the huge city was mysteriously abandoned around 750, possibly because of warfare and/or ecological destruction). The top affords a breathtaking view of the whole site, including the 45-m-high Pyramid of the Moon

The exquisitely carved Atlanteans of Tula were not discovered until the 20th century

(Pirámide de la Luna), which was built later and marks the end of the Causeway. As you walk towards it, be sure to examine the large coloured mural of a puma on your right. Beside the Pyramid of the Moon is the Palace of the Quetzal-Butterfly *(Palacio del Quetzalpapálotl)*, where there are more paintings. We may never solve the mystery of this great pre-Columbian city, as no written documents have ever been found on it.

As you prepare to leave, look around to see if there are any *voladores* by the exit waiting for enough spectators to perform.

Tula (166/C4)

This important archaeological site is only 90 km north-west of Mexico City and is famous because of the massive 4.6-m-high *Atlanteans*, which at one time were the columns supporting the roof of the Temple of the Morning Star and are now standing alone at the top, visible from the distance. The stone statues represent armed warriors and consist of four parts. They bear witness to the great skill of pre-Columbian sculptors. The site was not excavated until 1938.

We know more about Tula than about Teotihuacán: after the fall of the latter, a tribe that spoke Náhuatl settled here, calling the place Tollan, 'place of reeds', and slowly evolving into the powerful Toltec civilization. As you enter the site, look out for the large ball court *(juego de pelota)* measuring 67 × 12.5 m (a game the Indians took very seriously and popular amongst the Maya as well); from there, Tula's main attraction is seen immediately, the 10-m-high *Step Pyramid of* *Quetzalcóatl* with the world-famous Atlanteans.

Then walk down to the adjoining 'Burned Palace' *(Palacio Quemado)*. The walls of the central courtyard retain some of their original bright colour; in the centre are two Chac-Mool stone figures in whose central cavity the pulsating hearts of the sacrificed victims were placed.

MORELIA

(166/A4) Mexico's 'golden triangle' is formed by the cities of Puebla, Querétaro and Morelia. The capital of the state of Michoacán (pop. 800,000) is home to one of Mexico's most beautiful historical districts; all eight blocks have been preserved for posterity: impressive churches, finely restored manor houses, *plazas* bordered by trees and flowers and arcaded patios, most of them built with the ubiquitous pink sandstone, which greatly contributes to the beauty of the place.

The capital of the city of Michoacán lies 300 km west of Mexico City at an altitude of 1,900 m. Its former name of Valladolid was changed to Morelia to honour José María Morelos, the patriot of the War of Independence who drove away the Spaniards. The local university, the prestigious Colegio de San Nicolás, was founded in 1540 by Bishop Vasco de Quiroga and is one of the continent's oldest institutions of higher learning. Its most distinguished pupil was Father Hidalgo.

Morelia is surrounded by volcanoes of all sizes, which makes it one of Mexico's most beautiful and varied states. Even in the political arena, Morelia has played an important part: the former governor of the state and leader of the opposition party PRD, Cuauhtémoc Cárdenas, is now the mayor of Mexico City. His father, Lázaro Cárdenas, one of Mexico's most famous presidents, was born in Michoacán.

SIGHTS

Acueducto Colonial
The city's green pride, the carefully laid out Bosque Cuauhtémoc, is the starting point of the impressive, 1.5-km-long colonial aqueduct finished in 1785 that once brought the water from the surrounding mountains. Its 230 arches (arcos) of pink sandstone reach 9 metres in certain parts and are lit up after dusk.

Catedral
The Baroque cathedral, erected in 1640, received its Churrigueresque façade a century later and is one of Mexico's prime examples of this ornate architectural style. Particularly impressive are the portals. *Between the Plaza de los Mártires and the Plaza de Armas*

Palacio del Gobierno
This large palace, built in 1732, confuses the visitor with its maze of stairways, patios and arcades. The walls are decorated with numerous colourful *murales* by Alfredo Zalce, depicting scenes of the history of Michoacán. *Av. Madero Oriente*

Plaza de los Mártires
The city's lively main square is surrounded by colonial palaces, arched walkways and beautiful laurel trees. The colonial urban planners laid out the city's streets in grid-like fashion. Morelia's main street, the Avenida Madero, runs from east to west. Virtually all the sights are on it or a few blocks away from it.

MUSEUMS

Casa de la Cultura
♴ Built in 1619 as a Carmelite convent, the structure is one of the oldest and most important buildings in the city, and a magnet for art-lovers. The former convent houses an art gallery as well as temporary exhibitions of paintings and Indian masks. *Tues–Sun 10 am–8 pm, Av. Madero Oriente*

Casa de Morelos
This is the patrician house where patriot José María Morelos spent most of his life. He liked to sit on the patio to read and relax. *Tues–Sun 9 am–1 pm and 2 pm–6 pm, Av. Morelos Sur 232/Av. Aldama*

Casa Natal de José María Morelos
This is the house where Morelos was born. It contains many personal items as well as historical documents and a library. *Tues–Sun 9 am–2 pm and 4 pm–7 pm, Corregidora 113/Av. García Obeso*

Museo de Arte Colonial
In this old patrician home, the visitor has a wonderful opportunity to admire antique furniture and colonial art from the 16th to the 18th century, plus an interesting exhibition of old crucifixes and several sculptures made from the city's typical pink sandstone. *Tues–Fri 10 am–2 pm and 5 pm–8 pm, Sat/Sun 9.30 am–2 pm and 4.30 pm–7 pm, Benito Juárez 240*

Museo del Estado

Interesting exhibits show the Indian influence on Michoacán's culture. *Mon–Fri 9 am–2 pm and 4 pm–8 pm, Sat/Sun 9 am–2 pm and 4 pm–7 pm, Guillermo Prieto 176*

Museo Regional Michoacano

This overly decorated, large manor house dating back to the 18th-century houses not only the state's historical museum but an art gallery with beautiful colonial furniture as well. *Tues–Sat 9 am–7 pm, Sun 9 am–3 pm, Allende 305/Av. Abasolo*

RESTAURANTS

Attractive restaurants with open-air patios in venerable colonial buildings are the city's trademark. Especially attractive are the arcades of the Posada de la Soledad.

Cenaduría Lupita

❀ A family restaurant offering snacks and a good selection of regional fare. *Sánchez de Tagle 1004, Tel. 0143/12 13 40,* and *Av. Camelinas 3100, Tel. 0143/24 40 67, category 2*

El Churro

⚡ A bar serving tacos and other delicious delicacies, popular amongst the young crowd; highly recommended. *Lázaro Cárdenas 2279 (Col. Chapultepec Norte), Tel. 0143/14 42 55, category 3*

Fonda las Mercedes

The home and restaurant of the artist and chef Sergio Álvarez serves Mexican dishes in a room filled with fantastic masks, paintings, columns, palms and a drinking trough for horses. *León Guzmán 47, Tel. 0143/12 61 13, category 2*

Las Trojes

Lively family restaurant serving good regional dishes and specialities from the grill. *Juan Sebastián Bach 51 (Col. Loma Camelinas), Tel. 0143/14 73 44, category 2*

Villa Campestre

The elegant atmosphere and good wine selection are ideal for an unforgettable evening. Advance booking recommended. *Av. del Campestre 465, Tel. 0143/24 00 10, category 1*

SHOPPING

The arts and crafts of Michoacán are exceptionally varied and beautiful. For centuries, the *indígenas* have created wonderful woven articles, lacquerwork, wickerwork and ceramics; also worth looking at are copper wares and wooden articles.

Artesanías Regionales

Everything imaginable, from sweets to guitars and statues of saints can be found here. *Guillermo Prieto 40 (near the Plaza de Armas)*

Casa de las Artesanías del Estado de Michoacán

Of all the numerous shops in the city, this one is well worth a visit. The building in which it is located was a Franciscan convent in the 16th century; it also houses a first-rate permanent exhibition of arts and crafts. For those interested in purchasing some of the works, a shop sells the crafts on display. *Plaza Valladolid/ Av. Humboldt/Fray Juan de San Miguel 129*

El Carmen

Neocolonial style, a central location and friendly personnel ready to help make this hotel a favourite amongst the younger crowd. *30 rooms, Calle Eduardo Ruiz 63/Benito Juárez, Tel. 0143/12 17 25, Fax 14 17 97, category 3*

Catedral

This tastefully renovated colonial house with several galleries under a covered patio has an outstanding location, opposite the Plaza de Armas and the cathedral. *42 rooms, Ignacio Zaragoza 37, Tel. 0143/13 04 67, Fax 13 04 06, category 2*

Mansión Acueducto

Quiet hotel in a good location. Ask for a room with a view of the aqueduct! *37 rooms, Av. Acueducto 25 (Col. Vasco de Quiroga), Tel. 0143/12 33 01, Fax 12 20 20, category 2*

Posada Don Vasco

This establishment is conveniently located in the city centre; it offers comfortable rooms and has its own restaurant. *36 rooms, Vasco de Quiroga 232, Tel. 0143/12 14 84, Fax 13 60 38, category 3*

Posada de la Soledad

A unique experience: spend the night in a former 17th-century monastery, located in the lively city centre; suites with open fireplaces and a lovely patio with flowers and the soothing sound of splashing water from the fountain. *49 rooms, Ignacio Zaragoza 90, Tel. 0143/13 06 27, Fax 12 21 11, category 2*

Virrey de Mendoza

Charming hotel in the city centre, housed in a former 18th-century colonial mansion with rooms overlooking the cathedral and a splendid patio. *70 rooms, Av. Madero Poniente 310 (Plaza de Armas), Tel. 0143/12 06 33, Fax 12 67 19, category 1*

Tourist information

Inside the Palacio Clavijero *(Nigromante 79/Av. Madero Poniente, Tel. 0143/12 04 15, Fax 12 98 16, www.proturmich.com)*, a former Jesuit school built in the 1650s.

Pátzcuaro   (165/F4)

65 km west of Morelia lies the very photogenic Lago de Pátzcuaro, one of the most beautiful lakes in the country. Surrounded by hilly countryside and volcanoes, perhaps the only thing that might strike the visitor as odd is the profusion of water lilies. The fishermen with their original butterfly nets now only pose for photographers, as the lake has been overfished. Instead, they now carry tourists to the small island of *Janitzio*. Apart from souvenir shops and modest restaurants, the island boasts a giant ⚜ *statue* of José María Morelos. The hollow statue has stairs that lead to the top, from which a fantastic view of the surroundings can be enjoyed.

Only 3 km away is the small provincial town bearing the same name. With its well-kept, white-washed houses, it is the perfect example of rustic colonial architecture. Numerous houses have been converted into hotels and restaurants, boutiques and small shops. The majority of the Indians (Purépecha, called Tarascans by the Spaniards) make a living producing and selling their crafts.

Be sure to visit the *Plaza Vasco de Quiroga*, named after the Spanish bishop who unceasingly fought for the welfare of the Indians. Impressive houses border the square. A good place to spend the night is the colonial hotel *Mansión Iturbe (14 rooms, Portal Morelos 59 / Plaza Don Vasco, Tel. 01434/203 68, Fax 0143/13 45 93, www.mexonline. com / iturbe. htm, category 2)*.

PUEBLA

(167/D5) The more than two million inhabitants of this colonial city are proud of having the largest number of churches per capita. Located on a high plateau 2,162 m above sea level and 130 km east of Mexico City, it is easily reached via a scenic highway. Puebla is flanked by three massive volcanoes, snow-capped Popocatépetl and Ixtaccíhuatl to the west and La Malinche to the north. The city is also the headquarters of Volkswagen de México, the last place in the world where the legendary VW beetle is still being built and exported.

The large city centre, which was declared a national monument several decades ago, was carefully laid out like a grid by the Spaniards soon after it was founded in 1531. The tile industry, which is the continuation of an Andalusian tradition, gave the city its beauty and wealth. The industry is still alive and well, the beautiful Talavera tiles are a household name here and abroad.

Casa de la Cultura
The former bishop's residence houses a cultural centre and the renowned *Biblioteca Palafoxiana*, a most impressive library, the oldest in Latin America, with more than 50,000 volumes in matching surroundings, with old globes, maps, marble floors and hand-carved cedar bookshelves. *Daily, 9 am–6 pm, Av. 5 Oriente 5*

Casa de Muñecas
The 'Doll's House' is one of the most conspicuous houses in the city, built in the typical Poblano style, with its icing sugar-white façade. *Calle 2 Norte / Av. Camacho (near the Zócalo)*

Catedral
The Puebla cathedral is one of the country's largest and most important churches. The Baroque interior boasts plenty of marble and onyx, as well as beautifully decorated altars. The ⩗ tower affords a wonderful view of the city centre and of the volcanoes. *Southern side of the Zócalo*

Church of Santo Domingo
In the capital of tiles, it's only natural that the city's numerous churches are lavishly decorated with them. The interior of this church is adorned with blue-and-yellow tiles. The adjoining Rosary Chapel *(Capilla del Rosario)* is one of the most impressive and lavishly embellished in the whole country, a must! *5 de Mayo/ Av. 6 Oriente*

Casa del Alfeñique

The exterior of this house alone warrants a trip. The inhabitants call it 'almond cake house' because the bright blue and white tiles are set off against a background of red ones. Inside is the *Museo del Estado*, with a permanent exhibition of regional costumes, amongst other things. The upper floor has been left in its 18th-century state. *Tues–Sun 9 am–5 pm, Av. 4 Oriente 418/Calle 6 Norte*

Convento de Santa Mónica

Dozens of exhibition rooms document the secret life of the Augustinian nuns, who ran the convent (in spite of the secularization laws passed in the 19th century) until 1934. *Tues–Sun 10 am–4 pm, Av. 18 Poniente/Calle 5 de Mayo*

Museo Bello

Extensive display of very old Talavera tiles (some 400 years old) in a house that functions as an art gallery. *Tues–Sun 8 am–4 pm, Calle 3 Sur/Av. 3 Poniente*

RESTAURANTS

Puebla offers a unique synthesis of Spanish and Indian dishes, exquisitely prepared. Try the *chiles en nogada* (filled chillies in walnut sauce), also the very famous sweet-spicy *mole poblano* or — as a dessert — *Santa Clara camotes* (candied yams).

Fonda de Santa Clara

Tasty, traditional Mexican cuisine; two locations. *Av. 3 Poniente 307, Tel. 0122/42 26 59, and Av. 3 Poniente 920, Tel. 0122/46 19 19, both category 2*

Sanborns

Although part of a chain, the restaurant offers good Mexican food for a reasonable price. *Av. 2 Oriente 6 (pedestrian precinct north of the central plaza), category 3*

SHOPPING

Mercado Parian

This is the treasure trove for local arts and crafts, including pottery and tiles. *Calle 6 Norte/Av. 4 Oriente*

Plazuela de los Sapos

❖ This small *plaza* offers all kinds of antiques; popular amongst the locals. *5 Oriente/6 Sur (south-east of the Zócalo)*

ACCOMMODATION

Camino Real

A restored 16th-century monastery in the middle of the colonial city centre, with antique furniture and peaceful patios. *83 rooms, Ex-Convento de la Limpia Concepción, 7 Poniente 105, Tel. 0122/32 89 83, Fax 32 92 51, category 1*

El Mesón del Ángel

Puebla's smartest address, this Swiss-run hotel is in a modern building with large terraces and balconies. A beautiful tropical garden keeps the city noise out. Wheelchair accessible. *192 rooms, Hermanos Serdán 807, Tel. 0122/24 29 52, Fax 24 22 27, category 2*

Posada San Pedro

A colonial hotel with a pleasant atmosphere, centrally located and highly recommended. *76 rooms, Av. 2 Oriente 202, Tel. 0122/46 50 77, Fax 46 53 76, category 2*

Royalty

A comfortable hotel in a good location with parking. The hotel's own restaurant serves good food in a restored and modernized colonial building right on the *zócalo. 33 rooms, Portal Hidalgo 8, Tel. 0122/ 42 47 40, Fax 42 47 43, category 2*

INFORMATION

Tourist information

Casa de la Cultura, Av. 5 Oriente 3, Tel. 0122/46 09 28

SURROUNDING AREA

Cholula   (167/D5)

⚜️ The landmark of this small city of 31,000 souls only 8 km west of Puebla is the huge, grassy hill overlooking it. On the top is a small colonial church, from which the view is unforgettable. In 1931, archaeologists realized that the 'hill' was actually a huge, 65-m-high *pyramid,* the continent's largest. Only the western side has been excavated and rebuilt. It is possible to explore the foundations via tunnels *(Tues–Sun 9 am–5 pm).* Lovers of sacral architecture should see the little country church of ★ *Santa María de Tonantzintla,* with one of the most dazzlingly ornate interiors ever created by pious Indian craftsmen.

Cuetzalán del Progreso   (167/E4)

160 km north-east of Puebla lies the picturesque mountain village of Cuetzalán, centre of the Nahua and Totonac Indian communities, and surrounded by coffee plantations and a luxuriant vegetation, which offsets the Spanish architecture of this town founded in 1547. A recommended accommodation for the night is the *Posada Cuetzalán (22 rooms, Calzada Guadalupe, Tel. 01233/103 95, category 2),* a whitewashed hotel in the centre, decorated with flowers and a large veranda in front of the rooms. Small pool. Nature-lovers should continue another 5 km to the south-west and stay at the *Hotel Ecológico Villas Cuetzalán (7 bungalows, Carretera a Zacapoaxtla, km 5, Tel./Fax 01233/104 23, category 2),* located in beautiful, scenic surroundings, ideal for walking.

On Sundays, the streets of the old city centre fill with Totonac Indians offering their wares, such as woven belts and embroidered blouses. The best time to go is during the first week of October, when the patron saint San Francisco is honoured. The *Indígena* groups come down from the surrounding towns and perform their traditional dances — an experience that shouldn't be missed!

Pious Indian craftsmen decorated the opulent interior of Tonantzintla

Pico de Orizaba (167/E5)

Although the Popocatépetl is Mexico's most famous mountain, this 5,700-m-high volcano, also called Citlaltépetl, is the country's highest, lying between the states of Puebla and Veracruz. The attractive city of *Orizaba* (pop. 100,000) lies at an altitude of 1,300 m and is the starting point for hikes to the peak. Twenty kilometres further east lies *Córdoba* with buildings reminiscent of Andalusia, also worth a trip.

QUERÉTARO

(**166/B3**) This colonial jewel and provincial metropolis lies 1,850 m above sea level, about three hours away from Mexico City. The Andalusian architectural influence is strong: white, balconied houses and *plazas* decorated with flowers, shady patios, colonial mansions and elegant Baroque churches lure visitors. Querétaro is synonymous with Mexican history: on 19 June 1867, the ill-fated Habsburg Emperor Maximilian was shot by a firing squad at the Cerro de las Campanas, the 'Hill of the Bells' overlooking the city, despite numerous European protests. In his only three years as Emperor of the country, the 35-year-old liberal originally supported by the conservatives passed laws banning child labour and created the famous Paseo de la Reforma boulevard in Mexico City. According to legend, he gave each firing squad soldier a gold peso and shouted 'Viva México!' before being felled by the bullets.

Acueducto de Querétaro

In spite of its wealth, the city has had to struggle for water, even during colonial times, when in the 18th century the rich Marquis del Águila financed the building of an aqueduct in order to obtain water from a spring 2 km away from the city centre: 74 colossal round arches, some of them 30 m high, were built. After nine hard years of labour, the precious liquid arrived at the Santa Cruz convent and from there was piped to the houses. The impressive Querétaro landmark is lit every evening. *Calzada de los Arcos (eastern outskirts)*

Casa de la Corregidora

This house *(Palacio del Estado)* has played a prominent part in the history of Mexico. In 1810, it belonged to the mayor, whose wife, Josefa Ortiz, called La Corregidora, overheard one day that the Spaniards had received word of the independence movement. She hastened to impart the news to Father Hidalgo, the leader, who quickly rang the bells of his parish church in nearby Dolores Hidalgo late at night, calling upon the people to rise against the Spaniards. *Plaza de la Independencia*

Cerro de las Campanas

A small chapel half way up the hill reminds visitors of the fate that awaited Maximilian of Habsburg more than a century ago. On top of the hill stands a monument to Benito Juárez, the 'Mexican Abraham Lincoln' and opponent of Maximilian. *Av. Hidalgo (western outskirts)*

Colonial palaces and green plazas: Andalusian charm in Querétaro

Convento de la Cruz

⚐ This convent, dating from the 16th century, is one of the oldest buildings in the country. It has seven inner courtyards, and Maximilian welcomed its tranquillity. Today, it houses a cultural centre. *Av. Independencia (east of the centre)*

Convento San Francisco

An old monastery whose origins can be traced back to 1540 is today the *Museo Regional.* Beside the monastery stands the church bearing the same name. After dusk you can hear the music played by the bands on the *plaza* in front of it. *Northern side of the Plaza Obregón*

Teatro de la República

A historical theatre in the truest sense of the word, since it was here, in 1867, that a war-time court martial decided Maximilian's fate. Fittingly, 13 years before, Mexico's first national anthem was heard here. In addition, the present constitution was drawn up in its interior in 1917. *Juárez/Hidalgo*

Museo de Arte

The former Augustinian convent housed the federal building in later years (the reason it's also called Ex-Palacio Federal) and is now open to art-lovers. *Tues–Sun 11 am–7 pm, Allende 14 Sur*

Museo Regional

In the city where the independence movement started, this museum gives the visitor detailed information. It is housed in the old monastery of San Francisco. At the entrance stands a barouche that belonged to Maximilian. *Tues–Sun 10 am–7 pm, Corregidora Sur 3/Plaza Obregón*

Many restaurants serving good regional fare may be found particularly in and around Plaza de la Corregidora, some with outside tables; the more modest restaurants are around Plaza Obregón.

Comedor Vegetariano
Mexican cuisine and vegetarian dishes accompanied by music being played in the kiosk on the *plaza. Corregidora 130, category 3*

La Flor de Querétaro
High-quality local cuisine served in an interior replete with Mexican antiques. *Juárez Norte 5, Tel. 0142/12 01 99, category 2*

Fonda del Refugio
The tables are outside, and the locals praise the midday menu as well as the view of the Monumento de la Corregidora. *Plaza de la Corregidora, category 2*

Marisquería El Ballenato
❀ Fish and shellfish in all combinations; very popular. *Bulevar Zona Dorada, category 3*

ACCOMMODATION

Antigua Hacienda de Galindo
This is the large hacienda that Hernán Cortés had built for his Indian mistress Malinche — and, for this reason alone, it's worth seeing, although it's located 40 km south-east of Querétaro in San Juan del Río (a rented car is a must). The old hacienda is surrounded by a luxuriant garden and boasts a chapel inside. Large, colonial rooms furnished in colonial fashion. Accessible to the physically handicapped. *66 rooms, Carretera a Amealco, km 5, San Juan del Río, Tel. 01467/207 77, Fax 201 00, category 1*

La Casa de la Marquesa
This 18th-century palace was converted into a hotel in 1995 and quickly became the city's smartest address. Chandeliers illuminate the tiled patios and Moorish arcades with walkways. Antiques, oriental carpets and cloth draperies decorate the luxurious rooms. *25 suites, Madero 41, Tel. 0142/12 00 92, Fax 12 00 98, category 1*

Hacienda Jurica
Peace and seclusion in a picturesque setting are the main magnets of this former hacienda, accessible to the physically handicapped. Rustically furnished rooms, a luxuriant flower garden, pool and tennis courts. Horseback excursions to the surrounding countryside are offered. *182 rooms, 9 km to the north, Carretera a San Luis Potosí, km 229, Tel. 0142/18 00 22, Fax 18 01 36, category 1*

Plaza
Very reasonably priced but nevertheless comfortable rooms. Ideally located in the city centre, with a view of the *zócalo. 29 rooms, Juárez Norte 23/16 de Septiembre, Tel. 0142/12 11 38, Fax 14 37 00, category 3*

Señorial
Comfortable rooms and carpark. Good location for city sightseeing. Highly recommended. *45 rooms, Guerrero Norte 10-A/Hidalgo, Tel. 0142/14 19 45, Fax 12 46 65, category 3*

ENTERTAINMENT

Jardín de los Platitos
❀ Before dusk, you should already be there in order to get a seat. Every evening, *mariachi* and *ranchero* bands play folkloric tunes. *Av. Juárez/Universidad*

Tourist information
5 de Mayo 61, Tel. 0142/14 01 49, Fax 13 85 11

SAN MIGUEL DE ALLENDE

(166/A3) As if time had come to a standstill: narrow, cobbled streets lined with old Spanish colonial houses and balconies. And it's no coincidence, since 1926 this city of 90,000 souls built on a mountain slope at an altitude of 1,900 m has been listed as worthy of preservation. Long a popular destination for American and Canadian tourists, artists and students because of its colonial charm and mild climate, it's also the home of the renowned Instituto Allende. On 21 January, the whole town celebrates the birth of its illustrious son Ignacio Allende, the comrade-in-arms of Father Hidalgo.

SIGHTS

Convento La Concepción
This large, 18th-century convent is now the home of the art school El Nigromante, but visitors are welcome to the building. A chamber music festival takes place every year during the first two weeks in August. *Hernández Macías 75*

Instituto Allende
🏃 Its original name is Casa de Solariega, and it was built in 1734 by order of count Tomás de la Canal, its former owner. It is now a famous art and language school, offering many summer language courses. The large, attractive grounds include a beautiful garden, a café and a well-stocked library. *Ancha de San Antonio 20, Tel. 91415/ 201 90, Fax 245 38, www.ugto.mx/info_turi_gto/sma/allende/new.html*

Plaza de Allende
❖ The attractive main square of San Miguel is bordered by Indian laurels and many benches, and it is the ideal place to relax under the shade of the trees whilst admiring the colonial buildings and observing the daily life of this charming city.

Church of San Francisco
For every square a church: the small Plazuela San Francisco is dwarfed by the 18th-century church built in the ornate Churrigueresque style, of which the façade is one of the nation's best examples. The interior is neoclassical in style and houses some magnificent paintings. *Plazuela de San Francisco*

Church of San Miguel (La Parroquia)
San Miguel is the only major church in Mexico that was rebuilt by an Indian master builder who, in 1890, used drawings of the Ulm Minster in Germany as a model. It is built from pink stone and has many droll, neo-Gothic decorations. *Plaza de Allende (southern side)*

MUSEUMS

Casa de Don Ignacio Allende
The famous freedom-fighter and pre-eminent son of the city, Ignacio Allende y Unzaga (1779–1811), was born in this Baroque house. Objects relating to

Neon signs are banned in picturesque San Miguel de Allende, a town listed as worthy of preservation since 1926

the Independence movement and pre-Columbian artefacts are on display. *Tues–Sun 10 am–4 pm, Cuna de Allende 1 (Plaza de Allende, south-west corner)*

Casa del Mayorazgo de la Canal

One of the best examples of a colonial mansion dating from the 18th century; neoclassical façade. Inside, temporary art exhibitions. *Tues–Sun 10 am–4 pm, Plaza de Allende (western side)*

RESTAURANTS

Mesón Bugambilias

Beautiful garden patio with a fountain and music; international cuisine. Always busy. *Hidalgo 42 (near the zócalo), Tel. 01415/201 27, category 2*

Las Musas

Café de olla and cinnamon cake; after visiting the convent of La Concepción, an ideal place to relax under shaded arcades. *Hernández Macías 75, category 3*

Pancho y Lefty's

One of the favourite meeting places for tourists; the delicious dishes are accompanied by musical performances in the evenings. *Mesones 99, Tel. 01415/219 58, category 2*

ACCOMMODATION

There are a good number of hostels along the streets radiating from the Plaza Allende; in addition, holiday flats can be had at the *San Miguel Vacation Homes (Tel./Fax 01415/266 16)*.

Posada Carmina

The small, charming hotel in the very heart of San Miguel was once a colonial mansion; very romantic atmosphere. *12 rooms, Cuna de Allende 7, Tel. 01415/204 58, Fax 201 35, category 2*

La Puertecita Boutique'hotel

Colonial charm combined with modern and luxurious comfort in this hotel atop a hill, that affords good views of the city. *23 rooms, Santo Domingo 75, Col. Los Arcos, Tel. 01415/222 50, Fax 255 05, http://www.unisono. net.mx/lapuert, category 1*

Real de Minas

A comfortable hotel featuring tennis courts, a children's play area, a small shopping centre and a small, hotel-owned bull ring. *215 rooms, Camino Viejo al Panteón 1 (Ancha de San Antonio), Tel. 01415/226 26, Fax 217 27, http://www.unisono.net.mx/realm, category 2*

Villa Jacaranda

The colonial 18th-century manor house was built around a patio garden. Quiet location only three blocks away from the main square. Sip your aperitif whilst you listen to the soothing sound of a splashing fountain. The premises are equipped with a small theatre and a whirlpool. Wheelchair accessible. *15 rooms, Aldama 53, Tel. 01415/210 15, Fax 208 83, www.villajacaranda.com, category 1*

Tourist information

Palacio Municipal, Plaza de Allende, Tel./Fax 01415/265 65

Dolores Hidalgo   (166/A2-3)

About 40 km north-west of San Miguel de Allende lies the very famous village of Dolores Hidalgo (pop. 25,000). It was here in September 1810 that Father Hidalgo rang the bells of his parish church to announce the end of colonial Mexico. After admiring the *church* with its pretty Churrigueresque façade, continue on to *Casa de Don Miguel Hidalgo y Costilla*, where, from 1804 to 1810, the heroic village priest lived. It is now a *museum*, displaying exhibits of the fight for independence. After your visit, walk back to the *zócalo*, the ideal spot for relaxing. Needless to say, its official name is Parque Hidalgo.

TAXCO

(166/B5-6) ★ The silver city has impressed many a foreign visitor, amongst them German naturalist Alexander von Humboldt, who spent one night here in 1803. This highly picturesque city (pop. 150,000) is built on the slopes of the El Atache mountains and is at an altitude of 1,660 m. While walking through the ro-

---

Mordida – The 'bite'

Just like the Inuit, who have numerous words describing snow, Mexicans have many for bribery. Keep in mind, though, that the word does not always have the bad reputation of Anglo-Saxon countries, since without it everything in Mexico would come to a standstill. Underpaid workers are more than happy to get a 'reward' for their services, such as obtaining a permit or a certificate, call a taxi, get an appointment with a V.I.P. or even avoid an (often unjust) fine. Thus, the 'bite' is the lubricant needed for the smooth running of society.

mantic cobbled streets, you may hear the faint sound of the silversmith's hammer, a natural sound in a city that boasts almost one thousand *plateros* and more than 300 silver shops.

This colonial city, some 170 km south of Mexico City, is one of the nation's most romantic: white-washed houses covered by red tiled roofs with blooming jaca-randa trees and bougainvilleas, former manor houses, timeless narrow cobbled streets and historical fountains give visitors a feeling of being transported back to the 18th century, when silver baron José de la Borda (who was actually a Frenchman, but changed his name so it would sound Spanish) discovered a large silver mine. With part of the money he earned, he built the magnificent Church of Santa Prisca. His motto was: 'Dios da a Borda, y Borda da a Dios' – God gives to Borda, and Borda gives back to God.

SIGHTS

Church of Santa Prisca

The basilica, built of red sand-stone, can be seen from far away thanks to its 48-m-high twin towers. It is one of Mexico's most beautiful and has been the subject of many posters. The interior is lavishly decorated with gold leaf. *Plaza de la Borda*

Zócalo

Taxco's central square is named after its wealthy patron (Plaza de la Borda) and surrounded by co-lonial residences, amongst them the *Palacio Borda*, built in 1759 for Don José. It is now a cultural institute.

MUSEUMS

Museo de Arte Virreinal

This is a former inn where Humboldt spend one night on his way to Mexico City. It is still called Casa de Humboldt and is now a museum of religious art. Its façade is memorable. *Tues–Sun 10 am–5 pm, Juan Ruiz de Alarcón 12*

Museo Don Guillermo Spratling

William Spratling, Taxco's 20th-century patron, was an American who helped Taxco's silversmiths regain lost markets by bringing the craftsmen into the city and teaching them new techniques informed by pre-Columbian practices. The museum houses many exquisite silver objects and Spratling's own collection of pre-Columbian art. *Tues–Sun 9 am–4 pm, Porfirio Delgado 1*

RESTAURANTS

La Casona

This colonial house next to the cathedral offers a truly wonder-ful bird's eye view from the ⇖balcony. Enjoy delicious Mexican dishes while you ad-mire the hilly silhouette of this silver town. Friendly atmos-phere, reasonable prices. *Celso Múñoz 4, Tel. 01762/210 71, category 2*

Cielito Lindo

This Mexican restaurant at the Zócalo is always full. Breakfast also served. *Plaza de la Borda 14, Tel. 01762/206 03, category 2–3*

Sr. Costilla's

⇖With a nice view of the *zócalo*; particulary fine views

can be had from the balcony tables. Rustic interior. *Plaza de la Borda 1, Tel. 01762/232 15, category 2*

SHOPPING

Although the prices for silver are not really lower than in other places, the selection is infinitely better in Taxco. This precious metal, moulded by the patient hands of the silversmiths, is transformed into rings, earrings, chains, belt buckles and brooches, often adorned with coral, turquoise and mother-of-pearl. By haggling, you can sometimes lower the purchasing price by up to 30 per cent. It is certainly advisable to purchase any silver accessories from established shops by the *zócalo* and not from street vendors. By all means, make sure that what you are buying is real silver, not a second-rate imitation (ensure the object has the 925 sterling silver mark stamped on the back).

ACCOMMODATION

Agua Escondida
☘ For years, popular amongst individual travellers, this hostel in a colonial building is located on the *plaza* and has always been run by the same family. *50 rooms, Plaza de la Borda 4, Tel. 01762/211 66, Fax 213 06, category 2*

Casa Grande
Colonial house with a pretty patio and a bar/restaurant. *La Concha Nostra.* With a view of a small *plaza. 12 rooms, Plazuela de San Juan 7, Tel. 01762/209 69, Fax 211 08, category 3*

A gold mine for silversmiths: more than 900 plateros earn their living in Taxco's countless silver shops

Posada de la Misión
◁▷A colonial oasis in the middle of a luxuriant, peaceful garden. The terrace restaurant affords a fantastic view of the city (the food is also excellent). At the pool, you can admire a huge mosaic by famous artist Juan O'Gorman, which vividly portrays the history of Mexico. The city is best explored on foot from the hotel. *158 rooms, Cerro de la Misión 32, Tel. 01762/200 63 and 205 33, Fax 221 98, category 1–2*

INFORMATION

Tourist information
Here, one may pick up, for example, a list describing the various cultural activities and events offered in Taxco, especially the religious festivals. *Av. Presidente John F. Kennedy 28, Tel. 01762/ 215 25*

Swimming, sunbathing and snorkelling

*Inviting tropical beaches and coves await
water-enthusiasts and sun-worshippers*

Those who come down from the high, rugged Sierra Madre Occidental to the magnificent west coast experience the charm and beauty of this region first-hand. The road climbs first to high mountain passes, spans daring bridges over deep gorges, continues through cool conifer forests, which gradually give way to more subtropical vegetation, until the deep blue Pacific coastline with its white, sandy beaches and swaying coconut palm trees is reached. For many centuries this coastline was sparsely populated by a few fishermen; the coves often being the hideouts of British and Dutch pirates waiting to attack the Spanish ships. Nowadays, all kinds of coastal resorts have sprung up, although there are still plenty of hidden coves and bird-filled lagoons.

From Mazatlán, the old coastal resort located in the central stretch of the Mexican Pacific coast (it lies at the same latitude as Los Cabos, at the tip of the Baja Peninsula), all the way to

*The Romantic tropics
of the Mexican Riviera*

Huatulco, the new, southernmost resort, there are almost 2,000 km of magnificent coastline connected by the paved roads, MEX 15 and (from Tepic) MEX 200, as well as by dozens of airports, large and small.

Ever since the early 1940s, Hollywood began to discover the beauty of the Mexican South. In the beginning, it was the remoteness, being away from all the reporters and fans, that drew many well-known actors here; Johnny Weismuller and Errol Flynn being amongst the pioneers. First it was Acapulco, then in the early 1960s Puerto Vallarta, later the other resorts, such as Ixtapa/Zihuatanejo and Huatulco. Nowadays, the tourist industry can't do without these resorts, which are filled with expensive and tasteful resort accommodation, costly marinas and beautifully landscaped golf courses.

The area encompasses seven states: Sinaloa, Nayarit, Jalisco, Colima, Michoacán, Guerrero and Oaxaca. Of all the states, Oaxaca boasts the largest number of archaeological sites, but colonial charm is found in all, and it is precisely this combination of *zócalo*, historical city centre, and tropical beach that makes these coastal resorts so attractive.

ACAPULCO

(168/B4) Endless rows of hotels, restaurants and discos along the glittering Bay of Acapulco (one of the world's most perfect), million-dollar villas on the Las Brisas hill, cruise ships in the old harbour and bands of *mariachis* in the *zócalo*: this is the first impression one gets of Acapulco. From having barely 15,000 inhabitants in the early 1940s to the two million of today, the city has become the playground of both foreigners and Mexicans alike, attracting up to 3.5 million visitors per year.

It has often been said that Acapulco has no history, but this is not exactly true: none other than Hernán Cortés chose the ideal harbour as a starting point for his expeditions (to the Gulf of California, for example), thereby making Acapulco the centre of Pacific trade. During colonial times, the Spanish Manila Galleons would anchor here, their merchandise transported on mules to Veracruz, where the goods would be sent to Europe. No wonder Acapulco had to be fortified to protect it from pirates. After Mexico achieved independence, the port lost its importance; so much so, that in 1803 the German explorer and naturalist Humboldt thought it was 'small and sleepy', whilst on the other hand admitting that 'the coast couldn't be more picturesque'. Indeed, many would immediately agree with him. The beginning of the lasting tourism boom started with the opening of the airport in 1945.

After the resort lost some of its charm in the early 1990s, the city fathers invested heavily in parks, gardens and environmental protection. Currently, 'Acapulco Diamante', a large tourism project with hotels, golf courses and marinas, is being built.

SIGHTS

The Quebrada cliff divers

★ ↘↗ You have doubtless seen them in many posters: the daring divers jumping from the 42-m-high cliff called La Quebrada into a narrow, shallow cove. The *clavadistas* must time their jump well so they land when the cove is filled with water. The best view is from the terrace of the restaurant *La Perla* (*in the Hotel Glorias, Tel. 0174/83 11 55, category 1*), which is expensive

MARCO POLO SELECTION: THE WEST COAST

The daring divers of Acapulco jump from the famous cliffs of La Quebrada

(the bad food is part of the package), but a must; floodlit at night. *Daily 8.15 pm, 9.15 pm, 10.30 pm and a special show at 1 pm, admission (stairway US $1.30), at the western end of the historical city centre*

MUSEUM

Fuerte San Diego

This is the fort built by the Spaniards in the late 18th century to protect the city from pirate raids; it is now a museum specializing in the history of the Pacific pirates. *Tues–Sun 10 am–5 pm, Costera M. Alemán at the Malecón Fiscal*

RESTAURANTS

La Bahía

⤴⤵ Located in the Radisson Hotel, it offers moderately priced, good international and Mexican cuisine, with a splendid view. *Playa Guitarrón 110 (eastern part of the bay), Tel. 0174/81 22 22, category 1*

La Gran Torta

❁ Cook Laurentina offers refined Mexican cuisine and seafood specialities; many local families eat here. *La Paz 6 (near the zócalo), Tel. 0174/838 46, category 3*

Pepe D'

Mexican dishes, served fast by friendly personnel. Recommended dish: 'Mar y Tierra with wine' for two persons. *Calle Hernán Cortés 30 (near the Plaza Bahía), no Tel., category 3*

Rock It! Diner

Restaurant and bar with outdoor tables at the *zócalo*; not always quiet, but with a lively Mexican atmosphere. *Plaza Álvarez, Tel. 0174/83 09 87, category 3*

SHOPPING

Acapulco is not the ideal place to shop. Granted, there are countless souvenir shops, but the quality of their wares leaves a lot to be desired and the prices are uniformly high. The majority of the shops can be found along the endless Costera Miguel Alemán and, if that were not enough, street vendors people the beaches. At the corner of Horacio Nelson and James Cook (Costera behind the Baby-O'-disco) is the *AFA (Artesanías Finas Acapulco)* shop, resembling a large supermarket offering high-quality arts and crafts from all corners of Mexico. Be prepared to pay for the quality, however. Along the Costera, many American-style shopping malls have been built; a good selection can be found at Gran Plaza and Plaza Bahía (with affordable restaurants). Behind the *zócalo* are several streets filled with souvenir and arts-and-crafts shops.

ACCOMMODATION

More than 300 hotels and holiday flats of all sizes and prices await the visitor in this coastal resort city.

Las Brisas

This is still Number One in Mexican accommodation, and one of the world's best. The visitors' book reads like a *Who's Who*. Located high above the bay, the grounds occupy an entire hillside, boasting 300 luxury *casitas*, one-third of them with private pools. Electric, non-polluting small cars are used throughout the grounds. The whole complex is so paradisiacal that many guests never leave it, preferring to enjoy the good life within. *300 rooms, Carretera Escénica 5255, Tel. 0174/84 15 80, Fax 84 22 69, category 1*

California

☆ A *casa de huéspedes* (guest house) close to the *zócalo* with a quiet patio in the otherwise noisy city centre. Meeting place of the young crowd. *22 rooms, La Paz 12, Tel. 0174/82 28 93, category 3*

Continental Plaza

An elegant address frequented mostly by Americans. Rooms with terraces overlooking the sea; pools; attractive landscaping. Ideal for children (playgrounds, extra pool, children's club with programmes). *433 rooms, Costera M. Alemán 163 (city centre), Tel. 0174/84 09 09, Fax 84 20 81, category 1*

Days Inn

Situated in the eastern half of the bay, in the second row ($^1/_2$ block away from the beach). Rooms with balconies, some with a view of the ocean. *222 rooms, Costera M.*

Some 3.5 million tourists per year visit the resort metropolis of Acapulco

Alemán 2310, Tel. 0174/84 53 32, Fax 84 58 22, e-mail: acadays@ acabtu.com.mx, category 2

Del Magisterio
The colonial-style rooms surround the pool. Many Mexican families come here. *28 rooms, Hornitos 4 (off Costera M. Alemán towards Fort San Diego), Tel. 0174/83 21 52, category 3*

Beaches
Acapulco has many attractive beaches to offer. Favoured by the locals is the ✪ *Playa Caleta* (westernmost part of the bay) with numerous inexpensive beach cafés. The boats taking tourists to the *Isla Roqueta* depart from here; the island's beaches are quiet and less crowded. *Playa Hornos* (in the middle of the bay, opposite the Parque Papagayo) is the classical afternoon meeting place. You can enjoy almost constant sun in the easternmost beach of *Playa Icacos.* The *Playa Revolcadero* (15 km east of Acapulco Bay) is a long beach with fine sand, but don't swim too far out since this is open sea. Pie de la Cuesta, located 9 km north-west of Acapulco, is a less crowded beach with impressive waves (not recommended for swimming). Many come here in the afternoons to enjoy the fantastic sunsets.

Amusement parks
In the international children's centre, ✝ *Centro Internacional de Convivencia Infantil (CICI)*, many very creatively designed children's playgrounds and dolphin shows await the young and old alike; several restaurants *(daily 10 am–*

6 pm, Costera M. Alemán, in front of the Playa Icacos, admission US \$5). In the attractively landscaped grounds of the ✝ *Parque Papagayo,* there are several different fair attractions, such as a Ferris wheel and a miniature railway *(daily 10 am– 10 pm, free admission, Costera M. Alemán, opposite the Playa Hornos).*

✝ Starting at 10 pm, teenagers and 20-somethings begin their all-night disco tour; in the early morning, you can see them having breakfast in the cafés of the discos. Stroll along the lively *Costera Miguel Alemán,* where new discos are constantly being built and the older ones lure the crowd with new attractions. Those in search of more class can take the *Carretera Escénica* to the neighbourhood of the Las Brisas and dance in one of the discos with a wonderful view of the illuminated bay.

Aeroméxico
Costera M. Alemán 286, Tel. 0174/ 85 16 00

Tourist information
Costera M. Alemán 187, Tel. 0174/ 84 49 73, Fax 86 91 68, Mon–Sat 9 am–6 pm

HUATULCO

(169/F5) 'Paradise found again' says the slogan of the Mexican Tourism Office. What is meant are the seven bays along the coast of Oaxaca, better known as Bahías de Huatulco. And indeed a Pacific idyll awaits the visitor: white, solitary, tropical beaches. Until 1983, many of them could be reached only by boat, and were known only to insiders and the few fishermen living there. That year, a few luxurious hotels, an 18-hole golf course, an airport as well as a new town for all the workers and their families were built. Nowadays, the open-air, rustic building of the airport welcomes visitors. In the year 2010, Huatulco will offer as many as 30,000 rooms and lure up to two million tourists. Until then, the bays are still one of the most remote destinations of the Mexican Riviera.

The most built-up of all bays is the large Bahía de Tangolunda. Apart from luxury hotels, boutiques and various seafood restaurants, there is a golf course and a marina.

In order to supply the recently built tourist complex, only 2 km away from the beach the community of *La Crucecita* (pop. 7,000) was built in the Mexican style, with *plazas,* open-air restaurants and a lot of tropical greenery. In the newly created town, there are many reasonably priced restaurants, and taxis take you to the beaches. Even the old, existing village of Santa Cruz was spruced up for the sake of tourism.

SIGHTS

There is not much to see in Huatulco, apart from the wonderful beaches, underwater fauna and natural landscape.

Bahía de Chachacual

This bay, now part of a nature conservancy area, lies at the mouth of a river. A road crosses the coastal forest, where you can admire the huge *zapote* and *ceiba* trees, the skyscrapers of the forest. In a small community live Afro-American families, descendants of the slaves brought to the country by the Spaniards.

RESTAURANTS

It is recommended to book the hotel with meals included. Many of

Huatulco has remained untouched by mass tourism

70

them have more than one, and some serve outstanding food. Those who prefer to eat out, La Crucecita has many modestly priced restaurants around the Plaza Principal.

Casa Real

The kitchen of the Sheraton Huatulco Hotel is known many miles around: inspired nouvelle cuisine combined with the specialities of Oaxaca cooking make it a culinary must. Advance booking and formal clothes recommended. *Sheraton Huatulco, Tangolunda, Bulevar Benito Juárez, Tel.01958/ 100 55, category 1*

ACCOMMODATION

Five-star hotels are situated right on the beach, three- and four-star ones are behind them; nevertheless, they are all surrounded by lush, subtropical vegetation. The best accommodation is at the Bahía de Tangolunda; more modest hotels can be found in La Crucecita.

Caribbean Village

Built on a series of terraces overlooking the sea, the 12 pink buildings stand out from a distance. Arriving guests are taken to their respective rooms in small cars. The well-kept, luxurious grounds are highly recommended for families (playgrounds and children's activities); Wheelchair accessible. Shuttle service to the hotel's own beach club. *135 rooms, Tangolunda, Bulevar Benito Juárez 8, Tel. 01958/100 44, Fax 102 21, category 1*

Club Med

A large club village occupying 19 hectares and bordered by four white, sandy beaches; a wide variety of programmes typical of Club Med are offered, especially sports (archery, squash, putting, animation). English and French spoken; during the summer months, children's activities. *483 rooms, Tangolunda, Tel. 01958/100 33, Fax 101 01, category 1*

Gran Hotel Huatulco

A favourite amongst the individualists, it's also the right place for nature-lovers. Situated near the nature reserve, and only 20 minutes away from the beach. *32 rooms, La Crucecita, Av. Carrizal, Tel. 01958/ 700 83, Fax 702 84, category 2*

Royal Maeva Huatulco

Praised for being one of the best all-inclusive resorts. Three restaurants and four bars are available to guests, and theme evenings alternate every week. All rooms have a view of the sea, nightly entertainment. A mini club for the little ones. *300 rooms, Playa Tangolunda, Tel. 01958/100 00, Fax 902 20, category 1*

SPORTS & BEACHES

Horseback riding

A recommended address for escorted rides into the empty hinterland is *Rancho Caballo del Mar* at *Conejos Bay.*

Beaches

Those who seek lonely, romantic beaches should go to *Bahía de Cacaluta.* Rent a boat to take you there and spend the whole day under palms and bougainvilleas. Watersports enthusiasts prefer the bays of *El Órgano* and *Maguey.* The water is very clear, and you are away from the crowds.

Tourist information

*Bahía de Santa Cruz, Tel. 01958/
715 42, Fax 715 41*

Puerto Ángel   (169/F5)

⚓ Puerto Ángel (pop. 3,500) is the
preferred meeting place for backpack tourists from North America
and Europe. Small hostels line the
main coastal street, and the modest cottages *(cabañas)* and 'hammock hostels' (gardens where
guests sleep in hammocks) can be
found 4 km away, at Zipolite
beach. Only a few kilometres west
of Puerto Ángel lies *Mazunte*, a former Indian fishing village well
worth a visit. Measures to protect
the sea turtles have now been put
into effect. Accommodation is
available to tourists.

Puerto Escondido   (169/E5)

You can't say any longer that this
harbour about 90 km west of Huatulco is 'hidden', since for years
it's been attracting surfing fans.
The town of 40,000 souls is very
close to Puerto Ángel and easily
reached. Over the years, hostels,
guest houses and small hotels
have opened, accompanied by
restaurants and souvenir shops, so
Puerto Escondido is a well-estab-
lished holiday resort. The atmosphere, though, has remained
informal, the visitors younger and
prices are considerably lower than
in Acapulco or Huatulco.

Parallel to the bay is the main
street, the Avenida Pérez Gasga,
which serves as the town's promenade. On both sides of the
avenue are beach hotels and restaurants, shops for batik shirts and
blouses as well as Indian amulets,
favourite gathering places for the
young crowd. Palm trees provide
welcome shade from the hot sun
and street vendors offer hammocks
for sale, while children stare at the
foreign visitors. Small cafés offer
fresh pressed fruit juices and yes-
terday's newspaper. Behind Bahía
Principal are several smaller bays,
and those who prefer more solitude can go to the Bay of Zicatela
and watch the surfers.

Recommended is the *Beach Hotel Ines*, which is surrounded by
thick vegetation and only 1 km out
of town *(15 rooms, Playa Zicatela, Tel.
01958/207 27, Fax 204 16, category
2). La Sardina de Plata (Av. Pérez
Gasga 512, category 2)* is a fish restaurant, with a view of the ocean.

IXTAPA/ZIHUATANEJO

(168/A3) The two are always mentioned together; they lie about
240 km north-west of Acapulco,
and together have 55,000 inhabitants. However, apart from that,
they have little in common and
are a study in contrasts: for those
who find Puerto Escondido too
provincial this is the right destination – and can enjoy both. Ixtapa
is a modern, artificially created
beach resort with many luxurious
hotels along the wide sandy
beach, many of them hidden away
in the lush tropical vegetation
of their parks and gardens.
Boutiques and chic restaurants
dominate the scene.

Very different is Zihuatanejo,
only 7 km away and almost 500
years old, which was originally
settled by fishermen belonging
to the Purépecha (or Tarascans)
Indians of western Mexico. It is
believed that long before the ar-

rival of the Spaniards, they created what must have been one of the continent's oldest bathing resorts, even building a protective wall against sharks. The most important street is the *Paseo del Pescador*, the harbour promenade, particularly attractive at dusk, when tourists as well as locals stroll along it whilst contemplating a gorgeous sunset before enjoying their evening meal.

SIGHTS

As there are practically no traditional sights, the most popular sport in Ixtapa is *hotel hopping*, meaning going from one hotel to another by walking along the beach (in Mexico, all beaches are public) and comparing each hotel's lobbies, pools and well-kept gardens; here you enjoy the taste of a *café de olla*, there you savour a *piña colada* and, starting at 4 pm, it's happy hour time, when you get two for the price of one.

Marina Ixtapa
A microcosm of attractive bars and designer boutiques amongst canals, boats and expensive yachts. This 'perfect' resort of the Mexican Riviera couldn't possibly lack a perfect 18-hole golf course, naturally designed by the specialist Robert Trent Jones.

MUSEUM

Museo Arqueológico de la Costa Grande
The archaeological finds have finally provided ample proof of what many had long suspected, namely that Zihuatanejo had been a pre-Columbian place of pilgrimage, which had a sacred status for many kings. Many objects from the Tarascan culture. *Tues–Sun 9 am–6 pm, Zihuatanejo, Paseo del Pescador (at the mouth of the canal)*

RESTAURANTS

The selection is large: apart from the restaurants and cafés in the hotels, there are numerous other restaurants, whose specialities should be sampled. Zihuatanejo is somewhat cheaper than other resort towns; the best restaurants here are situated along the main promenade, the *Paseo del Pescador.*

El Mesón del Puerto
A footpath along Playa Principal takes you to several restaurants with outdoor tables under the shade of palm trees. Here, Dinorah and Miguel prepare exquisite fish and crab dishes, making this place a must! *Zihuatanejo, Paseo del Pescador, no Tel., category 3*

La Sirena Gorda
The morning catch determines the selection in this rustic, popular pub. The speciality is grilled fish, which is often accompanied by tacos and a cold, refreshing Corona. *Zihuatanejo, Paseo del Pescador 20A, at the pier, Tel. 01755/426 87, category 2*

Ziwok
This restaurant for demanding gourmets lies behind the Sirena Gorda; outstanding Mexican cuisine, highly recommended. *Zihuatanejo, Juan N. Alvarez, Tel. 01755/431 36, category 3*

SHOPPING

In Ixtapa, American-style shopping centres with air-conditioning and top-notch boutiques.

You can find Ralph Lauren and Calvin Klein creations for a lot less than in Europe. More than 400 boutiques have been counted, including those selling the highest quality Mexican arts and crafts. An example is *Varadero* (hand-imprinted cotton clothes) and *La Fuente* (Talavera tiles and glass).

In Zihuatanejo, most of the shops are situated along the promenade *(Paseo del Pescador)* and in nearby streets. An arts-and-crafts market, *Mercado de Artesanías,* can be found at *Calle 5 de Mayo.*

ACCOMMODATION

Ávila

Small hotel at the Paseo del Pescador, run by friendly hosts. Some of the rooms are attractively furnished with air-conditioning and a view of the sea (by all means see the room first!); direct access to the beach. *27 rooms, Zihuatanejo, Juan N. Álvarez 8, Tel. 01755/420 10, Fax 432 99, category 2*

Dorado Pacífico

Located right on the beach; all rooms with a view of the ocean, a large pool; ideal for children (extra pool and children's programme). *285 rooms, Ixtapa, Bulevar Ixtapa, Tel. 01753/320 25, Fax 301 26, category 1*

Villa del Sol

Hidden away under the coconut palms and bougainvilleas, this small and very exclusive hotel belongs to the category of 'small luxury hotels of the world' and has been featured in many magazines. Beautiful grounds, and nicely decorated rooms with Mexican art. *36 rooms, Zihuatanejo, Playa La Ropa, Tel. 01755/422 39 or 432 39, Fax 427 58, category 1*

Zihua Inn

⚑ *Muy típico*: in the middle of the picturesque fishing village; with swimming pool, clean rooms and a young crowd. *30 rooms, Zihuatanejo, Av. Los Magos/Palapas 21, Tel. 01755/438 68, Fax 439 21, category 2*

SPORTS & BEACHES

Fishing

Deep-sea fishing is especially popular amongst Americans. Marlin, tuna fish and sailfish are taken from the sea (and after the obligatory snapshot for the family photo album, returned to their home). The prices range from US $80 for a small boat to US $200 per tour.

Golf

The *Ixtapa Golf Club* is famous for its unparalleled beauty. The course takes the player through lagoons and green hills, all the way to Playa Palmar. The unusual thing about this golf course is its proximity to an environmentally protected area, where alligators may be seen. A swimming pool, tennis courts and a restaurant are beside the club house. *Green fees approx. US $35*

Beaches

Ixtapa's biggest plus is its many wide beaches with fine sand. Those who find the popular *Playa Palmar,* next to the hotel zone, too crowded and noisy can walk to the nearby *Playa Hermosa* to the south and enjoy this beach bordered by cliffs. In Zihuatanejo,

Playa La Ropa awaits swimmers with affordable water sports offerings and a good selection of beach restaurants. At the southern end of the Bay of Zihuatanejo is the very interesting *Playa Las Gatas,* a white beach formed by coral, offering the best opportunity for snorkelling. It is still possible to see parts of the pre-Columbian breakwater submerged in the sea, and, for a few dollars, you can take a boat to see it *(from the Embarcadero Municipal Zihuatanejo).* From Playa Quieta, north of the hotel zone, boats of the 'cooperativo' take tourists to the small, green *Isla Ixtapa,* uninhabited except for the iguanas and deer. The island's four beaches invite sun-worshippers, and the romantic beachfront restaurants serve fresh fish and exotic drinks. For lovers of underwater fauna, the best snorkelling is at *Playa Coral.*

Water sports
Visibility of up to 20 metres and more than 30 varied diving spots (amongst them, believe it or not, a submerged ship) contribute to making diving one of the most popular sports in the area. Countless businesses and large hotels rent out diving supplies and offer courses.

ENTERTAINMENT

The many bars and cafés start filling up before sunset. Those who would like a unique experience can book a *Sunset Yacht Cruise* on an illuminated catamaran, very romantic *(information in the hotels or call: Tel. 01755/435 89).* The younger crowd likes to meet in the ✰ *Christine,* the most popular of Ixtapa and nicely decorated, inside the hotel Krystal Ixtapa.

INFORMATION

Tourist information
Zihuatanejo: Palacio Municipal, Juan N. Álvarez, Tel. 01755/421 28, Fax 420 82; Ixtapa: kiosk at the Bulevar Ixtapa opposite the Hotel Presidente

MAZATLÁN

(160/B6) The biggest harbour between San Diego and the Panama Canal boasts the biggest shrimp fleet in the world, but it is also a popular holiday resort. Since it is not as well known as Acapulco, this city of 490,000 inhabitants is a much more affordable alternative to its counterpart. Actually, it is the holiday destination of choice for most northern Mexicans. Luckily, the pretty historical centre has been left mostly untouched by tourism. During the 19th century, the port was occupied by the Americans (in 1847) and the French (in 1864). Quite remarkable is the large *Malecón,* the four-lane beach promenade that almost encircles the entire city centre. The surroundings are fascinating: swampy lagoons replete with pink flamingoes and white cranes. North of the city, between the coastal highway and the beach, more and more comfortable hotels catering to American tourists are being built.

SIGHTS

Acuario
Mexico's biggest aquarium gives a very good idea of the fascinating diversity of Pacific underwater life.

Tues–Sun 10 am–6 pm, admission approx. US $1.60, Deportes 111

El Faro
◁▷Towering almost 160 m above the ocean, this is the world's second highest lighthouse. The long climb to the top is well worth the effort. *In the southernmost tip of the peninsula*

Mirador
Although the cliff divers of Acapulco are more famous, their daring colleagues of Mazatlán are just as eager to jump into the sea. *Olas Altas/Paseo Claussen*

RESTAURANTS

La Copa de Leche
◁▷ Make sure you get a table with a view of the sea! The typical and delicious specialities are fish dishes and the best (home-made) *tacos* in town. *Olas Altas 1220-A Sur, Tel. 0169/82 57 53, category 2*

Doney
Regional Mexican cuisine served in an elegant 19th-century manor house. Large windows provide a lot of light. *Mariano Escobedo 610 (historical centre), Tel. 0169/81 26 51, category 1*

El Marinero
❂This is arguably the best restaurant in Mazatlán as far as price and quality are concerned. Accompany your meal with tasty Pacífico beer, a local brew. Preferred by the locals. *5 de Mayo 97, Tel. 0169/81 79 82, category 2*

SHOPPING

Mazatlán Arts & Crafts Market
More than two storeys full of arts and crafts of all shapes and sizes.

Between *Playa Mazatlán* and the *Balboa Club.*

Shell Shop
Shells, shells and more shells in all colours, shapes, sizes, prices and degrees of workmanship can be found in this truly unique shop in the *Hotel Playa Mazatlán, Loaiza 202*

ACCOMMODATION

El Cid Resort
An ambitious, large-scale holiday resort occupying both sides of the street includes an 18-hole golf course, four swimming pools and numerous restaurants. Very luxurious. Accessible to the physically handicapped. *1,100 rooms, Camarón Sábalo, Tel. 0169/13 33 33, Fax 14 13 11, category 1*

La Siesta
A small, cosy hotel on the coastal highway with a restaurant in the inner courtyard. *57 rooms, Olas Altas 11 Sur, Tel. 0169/81 26 40, Fax 82 26 33, www.lasiesta.com.mx, category 2*

SPORTS & BEACHES

Right beside the coastal highway lies the beach of *Olas Altas*, which is less for sunbathing and swimming than for promenading and being seen. Endless cafés and restaurants line the beach. North of the city, beaches stretch for many kilometres. Water skiing, parachute sailing, sailing and windsurfing are just some of the water sports offered here. Many boats for hire at the *El Cid Resort (Camarón Sábalo).* A bargain is the boat trip to the nearby *Isla de la Piedra* with wonderful beaches and groves of palm trees. ❂ *Equestrian games* are held in the arena on *Gabriel Leyva (corner Insurgentes) every Sunday at* 4 pm. ☺ *Bullfights* are held at the *Plaza de Toros, Rafael Buelna (turn-off at the southern end of the Camarón Sábalo), also on Sunday afternoons.*

ENTERTAINMENT

In the large hotels, once a week the *fiestas mexicanas* are organized, including a buffet and music for dancing, interspersed with shows. Recommended is the *fiesta* in the *Hotel Playa Mazatlán,* where children also have fun. *Playa las Gaviotas, Tel. 0169/83 44 55,www.playamazatlan.com.mx*

INFORMATION

Tourist information
Olas Altas 1300 (above the bank), Tel. 0169/85 12 21, Fax 85 12 22, and Camarón Sábalo 333

SURROUNDING AREA

Mexcaltitán   **(164/B2)**
Called the 'Venice of Mexico' by many, this unique village, located on a flat island in the middle of a lagoon, is about 250 km south of Mazatlán on the road to Tepic. During the four-month rain season in the summer, its inhabitants take out their canoes and paddle instead of walk the few streets of the village. The modest, typical restaurants offer the usual fare with the exception of exquisitely prepared fresh crayfish.

San Blas   **(164/B2)**
The tropical, dense vegetation along the shore and around this small fishing village of 7,000 people south of Mexcaltitán has so far

escaped mass tourism. Proof of former colonial times is the old Spanish fort *Fuerte San Basilio* and the old *customs house.* The village attracts a varied crowd of tourists, mostly during the winter months: surfing enthusiasts from the USA and young people from all over the world on extended holidays.

PUERTO VALLARTA

(164/B3) ★ This resort was put on the map when back in 1963 Hollywood director John Huston filmed *The Night of the Iguana* in nearby Playa Mismaloya and Liz Taylor accompanied Richard Burton. In the meantime, it has become one of the most popular Pacific resorts, with more than two dozen golden beaches. In spite of receiving a million tourists every year, the atmosphere of the former fishing village lying on both sides of the Río Cuale (pop. 290,000) has remained typically Mexican: cobbled streets in the city centre, red-tiled roofs and wrought-iron balconies characterize the townscape. The tower of the village church is bedecked with a giant crown!

The development of holiday resorts has taken place to the north and along the coast. Apart from the typical sporting activities, rides into the jungle are offered. During the *hora feliz,* the bars and cafés at the *Malecón,* the beach promenade, fill with customers.

SIGHTS

Isla del Río Cuale
The five-hectare-large island attracts visitors on account of its numerous open-air cafés and res-

taurants as well as small arts-and-crafts shops. There's always a jazz concert or a poetry recital going on.

RESTAURANTS

Le Bistro Jazz Café
Guests sit outdoors in the garden under thatched roofs. Outstanding breakfast, good crêpes. *On the island at the Río Cuale, Tel. 01322/202 83, category 2*

Café des Artistes
French cuisine with a distinct Mexican flavour, but without loud music. *Guadalupe Sánchez 740, Tel. 01322/232 28, category 1*

Pipi's
🌀 An outstanding restaurant. Brunch is served on Sundays from 9 am to 2 pm. Live music. Very

popular amongst the locals. *Pipila/Guadalupe Sánchez, Tel. 01322/327 67, category 2–3*

ACCOMMODATION

Casa de la Juventud
Separate sleeping quarters for men and women. Most of the guests are American. *33 beds, Aguacate 302-A, Tel. 01322/221 08, category 3*

Frankfurt
Small but well-run hotel with pool; situated in the 'restaurant street' of the city. *12 rooms (also with kitchenettes), Basilio Badillo 300, Tel. 01322/234 03, Fax 220 71, category 2*

Posada de Roger
A Mexican-style hotel in the city and only one block away from the beach; pool and a large garden. *48*

Those afraid of the sea can enjoy the inviting pools of the beach hotels

rooms, Basilio Badillo 237, Tel. 01322/206 39, Fax 304 82, www. puerto-vallarta. com/posada, category 2

Some of the prettiest beaches include *Playa Mismaloya* (about 10 km south) and those reachable only by boat (for example with the yacht Sarape, 9 am from the marina), such as ★ *Yelapa* (with palm-thatched restaurants and luxuriant tropical vegetation).

Tourist information
Juárez, Tel. 01322/201 42, Fax 472 76, www.puerto-vallarta.com

Costa Alegre   **(164/B–C4–5)**
The coastal highway MEX 200 crosses palm groves and small fishing villages, leaving holiday resorts and hidden hotels behind. The 250-km-long Costa Alegre, between Puerto Vallarta and Manzanillo, has become the latest and most exclusive tourist region of the west coast. Countless islands and islets dot the glittering waters of the Pacific, and the refreshing breeze has a salty flavour. Majestic palm trees sway above the pristine beaches, and the sun shines nine out of ten days, even during the rainy season. The afternoon downpours are a welcome relief from the heat.

Lagoons provide a safe shelter for many birds and mammals. The Indians called the southern half the 'turtle coast'. For the last two decades, the bays of the *Costa Careyes* have been the destination of the international jet-set, who have built their private villas amid the luxuriant vegetation, hidden from view. The government of Jalisco has declared the coastal strip between Barra de Navidad and Chamela an 'ecological coastal region' and, in so doing, set the course for pure holiday bliss along the turtle coast.

The villages of ⚓ *San Patricio Melaque* and ⚓ *Barra de Navidad*, situated on a sand bank between the ocean and a lagoon, are an insiders' tip for the young, Bohemian subculture. Life runs its course in the palm-thatched hotels and restaurants, and the visitors take advantage of the wonderful surfing conditions offered by the sea. A recommended accommodation is *Hotel Bel Air (52 rooms, Carretera Barra de Navidad, km 53.5, Tel. 01335/100 00, Fax 101 00, category 1)* surrounded by a huge tropical garden and offering a very informal atmosphere. The large rooms (and private villas) are uniquely decorated with wooden chairs and terraces overlooking the sea. Also within the grounds are elegant boutiques, a riding stable and, believe it or not, a 'children's club'.

Manzanillo   **(164/C5)**
Situated on a peninsula between two bays (about 270 km south of Puerto Vallarta) is the sprawling resort of ★ *Las Hadas*, 'the fairies', extravagantly built in Moorish-Mediterranean style, with arcades, whitewashed houses, *plazas*, water fountains, marinas and a golf course. In this super-luxurious location, the movie *10* with Bo Derek and Dudley Moore was filmed. *(203 rooms, Tel. 01333/400 00, Fax 419 50, category 1).* Nearby is Manzanillo, a typical harbour of little interest (pop. 55,000).

Boundless solitude

Explore the rugged, high mountains with an all-terrain vehicle or the railway

Immediately beyond the city limits of Tijuana, the solitude begins. Lower California, better known by its Spanish name of Baja California, resembles a long, thin finger that juts 1,300 km into the Pacific Ocean. This huge peninsula, on average only 90 km wide, is a world by itself. This stark landscape, with many shades of brown on which thorny bushes and countless species of cacti grow amongst bare rock formations, gives the impression of boundless solitude. In contrast to the forbidding interior, the fauna seen along the two coastlines is extremely varied.

Those who travel to Baja California encounter small, remote missions surrounded by a few houses, date palm oases deep in the desert and solitary, isolated fishing villages. Even the Spanish conquistadors didn't stay here long. After the missionaries came the adventurers, and later a few writers, such as John Steinbeck, who, in the 1940s, described the unique flora and fauna of the mountainous peninsula and the Gulf of California in his book *The Log of the Sea of Cortez*. And nowadays? Ever since charter flights and small business jets have landed at Los Cabos international airport, this region has experienced a boom. Hotels, beach resorts and golf courses have mushroomed everywhere, yet, for much of the animal life, things have remained the same: for millions of years, grey whales have been coming here between December and April to reproduce. The mainland across the Gulf is just as exciting: the northern Sierra Madre Occidental awaits the visitor with its breathtaking gorges, particularly a canyon that is deeper, larger and even more spectacular than the more renowned Grand Canyon of Arizona.

BARRANCA DEL COBRE (COPPER CANYON)

★ Mexico's 'Grand Canyon' is the Barranca del Cobre, or Copper Canyon, an awesome gorge that plunges 1,500 m into the depths of the earth. And the journey to it is just as impressive: the 13-hour trip by rail from Los Mochis on the Gulf of California to Chihuahua, that is, from the coast

The cliffs of El Arco mark the convergence of the Pacific Ocean and the Gulf of California

81

to the mountains and highland steppes, costs a mere US $27 (first class). An observation car allows you to take in all the impressive, varied landscape. Needless to say, this is considered to be one of the most unforgettable train journeys in the whole world, as it goes from 0 to 2,500 m in one day, continuing to the semi-arid highlands of northern Mexico.

More than 39 bridges and 86 tunnels had to be blasted through the Sierra to lay the tracks for the 'Ferrocarril de Chihuahua al Pacífico', which wends its way through the rugged mountains. Completed in 1962, the railway uses the symbol of a running Tahumara Indian. Indeed, the Tarahumaras are known the world over for their impressive running feats. Many can easily run hundreds of kilometres. The 5,000 *rarámuri*, or 'runners', as they call themselves, live in the mountain gorges of the high Sierra. Most tourists can get a glimpse of them on the platforms of the railway stations, where they are seen selling souvenirs.

The starting point for the adventurous rail journey is Los Mochis (**159/E3**), a prosperous agricultural and business centre of 210,000 inhabitants on Mexico's northern coast. Since the train departs every morning at exactly 7 am, most tourists prefer to spend the night in Los Mochis. The best place is *Hotel Santa Anita (133 rooms, Leyva/Hidalgo, Tel. 01681/ 570 46, Fax 200 46, category 1)*. The travel agency inside the hotel can book the train journey for you.

From Los Mochis, the train first crosses the subtropical coastal plain, where sugarcane, vegetables and other subtropical crops are grown. Just 12 km from the Bahuichivo railway station (**159/F1**), which is 250 km from Los Mochis and about 1,700 m high, is the remote town of *Cerocahui* (**159/F1**) with 750 inhabitants. Following the street, and passing a *Jesuit mission* dating from the 17th century, a waterfall and abandoned mines, you will finally reach the Urique River, where the former *gold mine*, now a *ghost town*, is located. In the steep, inaccessible slopes of the canyons, hikers can run into pumas, coyotes, bears, foxes, wolves and deer.

At the railway station called *Divisadero Barrancas* (**153/D6**), 300 km away from Los Mochis and already at an altitude of 2,250 m, all trains stop for 25 minutes, enabling tourists to take in the fantastic and unforgettable view from the viewing platform. The walls of the three canyons that converge here plunge to a depth of 1,500 m. In Ojitos, 2,460 m above sea level, you will reach the highest point of the journey. Some 20 km farther down lies *Creel* (**153/D6**), with its 12,000 inhabitants, which is the centre of Tarahumara country. Apart from growing fruit, locals also work in the timber industry. Some 520 km towards Los Mochis is the town of *Cuauhtémoc* (**153/E5**), the centre of a large Mennonite community. The end of the journey is the capital city of *Chihuahua* (**153/E5**).

ACCOMMODATION

Cabañas Divisadero Barrancas
A rustic building situated at the edge of Copper Canyon; the view is unforgettable. Only 200 m away from the railway station. *52 rooms, Tel. 0114/15 11 99, Fax 15 65 75, category 2*

Margarita's Plaza Mexicana
A new hotel with a friendly atmosphere. *26 rooms, Creel, Calle Chapultepec, Tel./Fax 01145/ 600 45, category 3*

Misión de Cerocahui
Beside the mission church in the centre of the Tarahumara village, a small house built in a rustic style. *33 rooms, Cerocahui, 12 km away from the Bahuichivo railway station, Tel. 0114/16 65 89, category 2*

INFORMATION

Ferrocarril de Chihuahua al Pacífico
Méndez/24a Calle, Chihuahua, Tel. 0114/15 77 56, Fax 10 90 59

SURROUNDING AREA

Topolobampo   (159/E3)
Those who start their journey to Copper Canyon from Chihuahua and would like to continue to Baja California, it is advisable not to get off the train in Los Mochis, but stay on until it reaches the ferry harbour of Topolobampo (pop. 3,000), where boats depart for La Paz. This fishing village has had a very interesting past. In 1868, the young American engineer Albert K. Owen was so enthusiastic about the place and the landscape that he planned

The train stops where three canyons converge, enabling passengers to take in the view

the erection of a 'socialist metropolis of the West' and named it Topolobampo. In order to connect the new town to the highlands, four years later he designed the railway route through the Sierra Madre to Chihuahua and on to the USA. In 1881, he persuaded the Mexican government to give him land, and, eight years later, 300 adventurers arrived with the ship from New York. After building a hospital, a school, streets and attractive houses, the whole project collapsed in 1891, and only few remained in the new metropolis.

Nowadays, you can see some of his blonde descendants playing on the ✪ *pier*, or letting their paper kites ride on the ocean breeze. Looking up towards the hills, you can still see some once elegant Grecian-style villas with their columns, arcades and large verandas. Their present owners doze in the sun, whilst their houses crumble away. When you reach the ⤳ *Cerro de San Carlos*, you'll understand why Mr Owen was so enthusiastic about settling here: small rocky islands dot the ocean, untouched coves and white, sandy beaches. The town makes its living from the ferry, incipient local tourism and lobster fishing. Two modest hostels and numerous beach restaurants cater to visitors.

CHIHUAHUA

(**153/E5**) Here's a cowboy city straight out of the Wild West. Wealthy *rancheros* come to Chihuahua (pronounced Tshe-wa-wa) to settle their cattle business and often decide to spend a few extra days in the city. Tourists know of this 1,500-m-high city because it's the terminus of the train journey. But this attractive city of one million inhabitants is also the prosperous capital of Mexico's largest state. Apart from boasting some wonderfully restored colonial palaces, it also has a good many elegant buildings in the Art Nouveau style.

Chihuahua is also the place where the legendary Pancho Villa was born, the most enigmatic and feared of all the revolutionaries. With his battle cry 'Viva la Revolución', he led his famous División del Norte to one victory after another, greatly contributing to the overthrow of dictator Porfirio Díaz. However, when some of his followers began to raid large landholders, he made many enemies. Eventually, he was shot, on 20 July 1923, after he had retired.

Catedral

Chihuahua's past wealth is evident in the 18th-century cathedral, built in the Baroque style with money from the silver tax. The magnificent interior is richly adorned. *Plaza Principal (also Plaza de Armas)*

Palacio del Gobierno

Imposing *murales* by painter Piña Mora dealing with the history of the state decorate this palace, built in the late 19th century. It was here, in the early 1800s, that the Father of Independence, Miguel Hidalgo, was executed by the Spaniards. A monument and his grave remind the visitor of the historical significance of the place. *Plaza Hidalgo*

Teatro de los Héroes

With its 1,400 seats, this modern theatre is the state's showpiece. In the ❀ ⚊ park in front of the building, young people meet and families can be seen picnicking. *División del Norte/Calle 23*

MUSEUMS

Casa de Juárez

This building served as the seat of government (only for a short period) during Benito Juárez's presidency. Only recently opened to visitors, the building houses interesting historical objects and personal articles. *Tues–Sun 10 am–5 pm, Juárez/Calle 5*

Centro Cultural Quinta Gameros

This house, a fine example of how the city's affluent once built, offers the rare opportunity to see the interior of a patrician home. The house of a well-known mining engineer is graced with elegant furniture, some of it in the Art Nouveau style. In addition, the cultural centre houses an interesting exhibition on the Mennonites. *Tues–Sun 9 am–7 pm, Paseo Bolívar 401/Calle 4*

Museo de la Revolución

'Quinta Luz' was the name that legendary revolutionary Pancho Villa gave to his 50-room palace, to honour the name of his recently deceased third wife. He lived here for nine years, until 1923, the year he was shot. *Tues–Sun 9 am–1 pm and 3 pm–7 pm, Calle 10 Norte No. 3014*

RESTAURANTS

Chalet Italiano

Italian cuisine; very popular amongst the local bourgeoisie. *Escorza/Calle 13a, Tel. 0114/16 0 9 40, category 2*

Fiesta de Mariscos

The name describes exactly what you get: fish and shellfish in all variations, all quite spicy. *Juárez 521, no Tel., category 3*

Rincón Mexicano

Regional and Mexican cuisine; in the evenings, a group of *mariachis* provides lively background music. *Av. Cuauhtémoc 2224, Tel. 0114/11 15 10, category 2*

SHOPPING

Mercado de Artesanías

The most important arts-and-crafts market. *Victoria 506 and Aldama 519*

ACCOMMODATION

Apolo

The city's oldest hotel is a four-storeyed building in the city centre, with a cafeteria and a friendly atmosphere. *43 rooms, Av. Juárez 907, Tel. 0114/16 11 00, Fax 16 11 02, category 3*

Camino Real

The youngest hotel in the city is also the best. A modern, functional building is surrounded by gardens, away from the city centre. Wheelchair accessible. *204 rooms, Av. Barranca del Cobre (Fracción Barrancas), Tel. 0114/29 29 29, Fax 29 29 00, category 1*

INFORMATION

Tourist information

Patio central, Palacio del Gobierno, Libertad/V. Carranza, Tel. 0114/10 10 77, Fax 15 91 24

Mennonite colonies (153/E5)

A visit to the city of Cuauhtémoc, about 100 km west of Chihuahua, gives visitors a taste of the Old World. Most of the approximately 40,000 Mennonites living here and in the surrounding farms have blonde hair and blue eyes, and they still speak an old German dialect. Back in 1921/22, shortly after the Revolution, about 500 Mennonites reached their destination: the enormous Hacienda Bustillos with its 100,000 hectares of land, bought from the Mexican government for two million dollars. In the meantime, their numerous descendants worked magic with the arid steppe, slowly converting it into small, tidy plots surrounded by undulating wheat. Visitors are politely greeted, but in a reserved way.

Traditional living: a Mennonite carriage near Cuauhtémoc

LOS CABOS

(159/D6) The once sleepy fishing village of Cabo San Lucas now boasts 12,000 inhabitants; it is strategically situated in the extreme southern tip of the Baja Peninsula, exactly where the waters of the Gulf of California (Mar de Cortés) and the Pacific meet. The austere beauty of the natural surroundings is truly awe-inspiring. On the cultural front, the visitor will look in vain for Indian and colonial Mexico. Cabo San Lucas resembles an oasis in the middle of an utterly dry and unpopulated landscape. This not particularly attractive town is in the middle of an economic boom: here a new hotel,

there a recently opened restaurant or shop, catering mostly to wealthy American deep-sea fishermen.

San José del Cabo, on the other hand, has retained a well-kept appearance. Its history dates back to 1535, when Cortés landed here. Later, it became a favourite haunt of English pirates. The town itself was founded later, in the 18th century. This small city of 30,000 souls is much more placid than the similarly named Cabo San Lucas, 30 km to the south-west. Some good restaurants and cafés can be found on Bulevar Mijares, the city's main street. Together with Cabo San Lucas, this up-and-coming resort region is called Los Cabos ('the capes'), and its busy international airport is an important destination for charter flights from the USA.

El Arco

A few experienced globetrotters will instantly recognize a photo of

El Arco, the unique offshore rock formation resembling a giant arch and marking the precise point at which the Pacific Ocean meets the Gulf of California. The city's landmark can be seen from the mainland, and many boat tours to the impressive formation leave from the harbour.

Estero de San José

This fresh-water lagoon, surrounded by extensive swamps, has been declared a *bird sanctuary*, where more than 250 species, amongst them pelicans and golden eagles, are protected. A short walk leads to the fishing village of La Playita, which is presently being converted into a resort. *Bahía de San José del Cabo*

Faro de Cabo Falso

A journey to this lighthouse, on horseback, makes for an adventurous day trip.

Whale-watching

The small boats carefully approach the gentle ocean giants until they are only a few metres away. Only in the winter do the grey whales plough through the warm waters of the southern half of the peninsula, when it's the 'season'. *Boat excursions organized by the Amigos del Mar association can be booked in major local hotels and travel agencies.*

Zócalo

The small central square of San José del Cabo looks very Mexican, surrounded by some attractive buildings. Beside the *Palacio Municipal* is the little *church of San José*, which, despite having been built in the mid-20th century, attracts many visitors. On the small *zócalo* stage, regular music concerts delight the tourist and local alike.

RESTAURANTS

Le Bistro

This is the place for a relaxed breakfast or a snack while exploring the city. *San José del Cabo, Morelos 4, category 3*

Damiana

This wonderful 19th-century manor house with its beautiful patio surrounded by climbing plants has been converted into a luxurious restaurant, and it's a favourite amongst American deep-sea fishermen. Outstanding fish dishes; steak is also a house speciality. *San José del Cabo, Bulevar Mijares 8, Tel. 01114/204 99, category 1*

Las Palmas

The perfect location, overlooking El Arco. Well known for its steak and fish specialities. *Playa El Médano, Tel. 01114/304 47, category 1*

La Placita

Large selection of fish dishes. *Cabo San Lucas, Bulevar Marina/Guerrero, Tel. 01114/300 30, category 2*

ACCOMMODATION

CREA Youth Hostel

Since even the modest guest houses are disproportionately expensive, the youth hostel is recommended. *164 beds, Cabo San Lucas, Av. de la Juventud, Tel. 01114/ 301 48, category 3*

Finisterra

⬥⬥ True to its name of 'Land's End', it's at the peninsula's southernmost tip. You can walk to the Playa del Amor and admire El Arco. *28 rooms, Bahía Cabo San Lucas, Tel. 01114/333 33, Fax 305 90, category 1*

Las Margaritas Inn

The ideal accommodation for those who wish to look after themselves: centrally located; suites with kitchenettes; meeting place of young American fishermen. *28 rooms, Cabo San Lucas, Lázaro Cárdenas/Zaragoza (Plaza Aramburo), Tel. 01114/325 50, Fax 304 50, category 2*

Punta Palmilla

Quite simply the very best hotel on the whole peninsula. In a fantastic setting amongst cliffs and palm trees, the resort hotel, built like a hacienda, boasts a well-known diving school and an 18-hole golf course designed by Jack Nicklaus. The suites have an open fireplace and are decorated with Talavera tiles. *70 rooms, Carretera San José del Cabo–Cabo San Lucas, km 27.5, Tel. 01114/450 00, Fax 551 00, category 1*

Westin Regina Los Cabos

The place for those who love modern Mexican architecture: famous architect Javier Sordo Madaleno created an arrangement with simple forms and bright, strong colours that sets this hotel apart from all others. The semicircular main building lies on the cove amongst the cliffs, behind it are terraced gardens, swimming pools and pink sleeping quarters. *305 rooms, Carretera Cabo San Lucas–San José del Cabo, km 22.5, Tel. 01114/290 50, Fax 290 40, category 1*

SPORTS & BEACHES

Between Cabo San Lucas and San José del Cabo are numerous beautiful, inviting beaches. Surfers prefer the *Costa Azul* and *Acapulquito* because of the large waves. *Punta Palmilla* is ideal for snorkelling, swimming and sunbathing. At *Playa Palmilla*, you can also find a shop that sells diving equipment and supplies.

Golf

Golf is the new, popular sport in Los Cabos. There are a number of wonderful 18-hole, award-winning golf courses designed by Jack Nicklaus and Robert Trent Jones. The best are *Palmilla, Cabo Real* and *Cabo del Sol.* These are also adapted to the needs of the physically handicapped. More are being planned.

Deep-sea fishing

The southern tip of Baja California is one of the preferred destinations of the world's deep-sea fishermen. Many world records have been broken here, and contests are held often. The hotels in the so-called 'marlin metropolis' of the world (Cabo San Lucas) also offer deep-sea fishing excursions – expensive!

ENTERTAINMENT

Cabo Wabo

Tequila and Mezcal can be had under an imitation lighthouse, stylishly fashioned. Different bands play from one day to the next. *Cabo San Lucas, Vicente Guerrero/Lázaro Cárdenas*

Lukas

♣ Disco offering an extensive music programme and lots of dancing. *Cabo San Lucas, Bulevar Marina (Plaza Bonita Mall)*

INFORMATION

Aeroméxico San José
Zaragoza/Hidalgo, Tel. 01114/ 203 98

Tourist information
Cabo San Lucas
Hidalgo/Madero, Tel. 01114/341 80, Fax 322 11

Tourist information San José
Obtain the free brochure 'Los Cabos – Inside', which contains many helpful tips and addresses. *Palacio Municipal, Tel. 01114/200 13*

SURROUNDING AREA

La Paz   (158/C4)
The capital (pop. 170,000) of Southern Baja California presents itself to the visitor with a modern face and many shops, restaurants, movie theatres and discos. The much more reasonable prices (compared to Cabo San Lucas) attract many young American deep-sea fishermen. The capital's hotels are less elegant and the beaches not as beautiful. Nevertheless, La Paz is definitely worth an extended visit. A relaxed tour of the city can easily take up a whole day, starting with the Anthropology Museum (which displays interesting photos concerning the history of the peninsula), continuing with the mural adorning the large wall of the city hall and proceeding with a stroll along the *malecón*. At the harbour, glass-bottom boats take tourists to small nearby islands and to the sea lion colonies. A good place to eat is the restaurant *Eneka (Madero 1520, Tel. 01112/546 88, Fax 241 06, category 2)*, which also offers reasonable accommodation.

Loreto   (158/B2)
The shimmering, azure water, solitary beaches and the imposing mountains of the Sierra de la Giganta make this village one of the peninsula's preferred destinations. With its 17,000 inhabitants, Loreto

The 1,000-km-long MEX 1 traverses the peninsula's solitary desert landscape

lies on the east coast approximately 500 km north of Cabo San Lucas. It was once California's first capital and, in the 19th century, three Welsh brothers named Davis started a clan; a street is named after them. A few years ago, director James Cameron chose Loreto to film many of the exterior scenes of his movie *Titanic*. The ship's replica has since been dismantled.

The church of *Nuestra Señora de Loreto* is Baja California's oldest, erected in 1697, the same year that the famous missionary Eusebio Kino landed on the coast and founded a small mission. Jeep excursions take you to the *Sierra de la Giganta* and the *San Javier mission church*. At Nopoló Bay (approx. 7 km farther south) lies *Diamond Resort (60 rooms, Tel. 01113/306 12, Fax 303 77, category 2)*.

San Carlos (158/B3)

★ ⇘ It is well known to biologists and oceanographers that since time immemorial grey whales have chosen the waters off the Baja Peninsula between mid-January and mid-April to reproduce, in effect using the waters as a giant nursery. Many of the observation points built for watching these impressive mammals are somewhat difficult to reach because the roads leading to them are either unpaved or non-existent. Nevertheless, it is easy to reach the observation points along the Bahía Magdalena, about 400 km north of Cabo San Lucas, on the western coast: San Carlos (accessible via Ruta 22), Punta Stern (about 1.5 km south of San Carlos) and the Puerto López Mateos (reached via a gravel road north of Ruta 22).

TIJUANA

(150/A1) It is easy to reach the Mexican border from San Diego: you take a modern suburban train to the world's busiest border, cross it on foot and you are in Tijuana, with its two million inhabitants, Baja California's biggest city. For many Californians, Tijuana is a favourite weekend destination. This bustling city offers wonderful shopping (the free trade zone along the border ensures low prices) and all kinds of entertainment (bars, restaurants, cabarets and gambling dens) guarantee the city's prosperity.

Maquiladoras

This is the name given to the numerous in-bond plants along the U.S.-Mexican border, owned mostly by American companies, but Japanese and Korean plants can also be found. The assembly plants profit from perennially low Mexican wages, and their number is huge: approximately 2,000 of these plants employing a total of 600,000 workers have been built along the border, but most can be found in Ciudad Juárez and Tijuana. In the morning, the lorries bring the parts to the plants, which are then assembled by Mexicans into complete articles (electronic goods, tennis rackets, clothes, etc.). In the evening, the lorries take the finished products back: a practical, albeit somewhat controversial, arrangement between the two countries.

Tijuana experienced its first boom during Prohibition. The 'world's longest bar', the Avenida Revolución, became the meeting place of the thirsty from Seattle to San Diego.

SIGHTS

Centro Cultural
❁ A multimedia show about the country and its inhabitants, plus archaeological finds and instructive exhibitions; in addition, folk dances and plays. Wheelchair accessible. *Paseo de los Héroes/Mina*

MUSEUMS

Mexitlán
Two hundred true-to-scale models of the most important buildings and pyramids in Mexico. *Daily 10 am–5 pm, Av. Benito Juárez 8991*

Museo de Cera
One of the only two waxworks museums in Latin America, it houses 60 famous personalities from history and Hollywood. *Daily 10 am–7 pm, 1a Calle 8281 (between Madero and Revolución)*

RESTAURANTS

Tex-Mex cuisine (Americanized Mexican dishes served in gigantic portions) dominates the menus.

Hard Rock Café
🕏 A few decibels louder than its neighbours; tasty dishes. *Av. Revolución 520, Tel. 0166/85 25 13, category 2*

El Jaguar
Includes a gallery and a bazaar in an elegant setting. *Paseo de los Héroes 10501 (Lincoln Circle), Tel. 0166/34 67 81, category 1*

El Lugar Vegetariano
A vegetarian oasis amongst all the steak houses. *Centro Comercial Las Américas 13, Av. Las Américas 3023, Tel. 0166/82 75 70, category 3*

SHOPPING

Avenida Revolución
More than ten blocks long is the chain of shops offering Mexican souvenirs, textiles and electronics for sale. Arts and crafts can be found around the corner, at 2a Calle.

Plaza Fiesta
❁ More than 20 shoe shops, plus various restaurants, attract tourists of many nationalities. *Paseo de los Héroes 1001*

ACCOMMODATION

La Mesa Inn
A comfortable motel featuring rooms with balconies, away from the city centre. *122 rooms, Bulevar Díaz Ordaz 50/Gardenias, Tel. 0166/81 65 22, Fax 81 28 71, category 2*

Pueblo Amigo
A modern facility close to the border, not far from the city centre. Indoor swimming pool and a good lobby restaurant. *108 rooms, Vía Oriente 9211 (Zona Río), Tel. 0166/83 50 30, Fax 83 50 32, category 1–2*

INFORMATION

Tourist information
Av. Revolución/1a Calle, Tel. 0166/84 05 37, Fax 81 95 79, Mon–Sat 9 am–7 pm, Sun 10 am–5 pm

Where tradition lives on

Old Mexico remains alive in Indian villages and in the markets of magnificent colonial cities

In the southern part of the country, from the state of Oaxaca all the way to Chiapas and the Guatemalan border, Indian traditions and folklore remain very much alive, and the visitor almost has the feeling of stepping back into colonial times. In the narrow, isolated valleys of the Sierra Madre in Chiapas live the direct descendants of the Maya, the 150,000 Tzeltal and Tzotzil Indians, who still speak their own language and can be distinguished by their colourful costumes. In the steamy lowlands crossed by the River Usumacinta, which at times divides Mexico from Guatemala, live a few scattered Lacandon Indians, the other descendants of the Maya. They consciously avoid contact with the whites and still use the same ancient slash-and-burn method of cultivation as their ancestors.

In Chiapas, '… the farmers are Indians, and the Indians are farmers. Here, the agrarian reform didn't take place; here, the

At Mitla, the Mixtecs used 100,000 stones to create unique geometric reliefs

land was not only not given back to the farmers, but the local oligarchy even took more land away from them', wrote famed Carlos Fuentes in all the world's newspapers — a masterly study of the Indian revolt of 1994/95. In reality, this was only the last and largest of a series of conflicts between the large private landholders (less than 100 families own most of the land) and the Maya descendants, who live in abject poverty.

In neighbouring Oaxaca, the situation is slightly better, but not by much. Here, as in Chiapas, tradition runs deep; the high mountains contribute to the relative isolation of many Indian communities, and also to their poverty. Catering to tourists is a means of alleviating their daily lives and providing the necessary jobs for their exploding population. Slowly, nature preserves have been expanded and hostels have been built in the typical adobe style with clay bricks. From the artistic and historical point of view, these two states are Mexico's veritable treasure: not only are such first-rate archaeological sites as Monte Albán, Mitla and Palenque here, but also important and well-preserved colonial cities with splendid Baroque churches.

Many centuries ago, the Maya founded their cities and ceremonial centres in Chiapas (as well as in the Yucatán Peninsula, Guatemala and Honduras), many of which still remain concealed by the thick, tropical vegetation, their remote location contributing to their protection against looters and grave-diggers who all too often arrive before the archaeologists. Ironically, Chiapas and Oaxaca are not only some of the most interesting and beautiful states in all of Mexico, but they are also the poorest.

OAXACA

(169/F4) ★ Many visitors come to Oaxaca (pop. 260,000) to use the city as a base for day trips to neighbouring pre-Columbian sites, such as Monte Albán, one of the most impressive of all. Those who can afford to do so,

Arcades and atmosphere in Oaxaca

stay a few days longer in this colonial capital city, which has managed to retain a contemplative, provincial and very relaxing atmosphere. Its urban architecture with its straight, carefully laid out streets, *plazas*, one-storeyed houses with inner patios and splendid churches from colonial times contrasts with the countless Mixtec and Zapotec Indians, seen wearing their colourful costumes, who have come down from their mountain villages to offer their varied wares for sale. Are we really in the 21st century? To ponder this question and discuss the many contrasts encountered in one day, the numerous restaurants and cafés surrounding the shady *zócalo* provide the perfect setting. In fact, at times you hear more foreign languages than Spanish or Indian tongues.

SIGHTS

Andador Macedonio Alcalá
From the central square, this pedestrian precinct bordered by great colonial buildings (some of them converted into restaurants and shops) takes you a few blocks northwards to the Church of Santo Domingo. On the way, you can admire the *Faculty of Law* of the University of Oaxaca, the *Library* and the small *Museum of Contemporary Art. Between the zócalo and the Church of Santo Domingo*

Plaza Principal
A tranquil *zócalo* bordered by cafés and restaurants under the arcades; daily concerts or marimba music are played on the round bandstand. The *Palacio de*

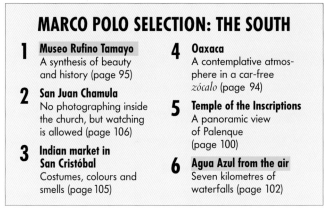

MARCO POLO SELECTION: THE SOUTH

1 Museo Rufino Tamayo
A synthesis of beauty
and history (page 95)

2 San Juan Chamula
No photographing inside
the church, but watching
is allowed (page 106)

**3 Indian market in
San Cristóbal**
Costumes, colours and
smells (page 105)

4 Oaxaca
A contemplative atmos-
phere in a car-free
zócalo (page 94)

5 Temple of the Inscriptions
A panoramic view
of Palenque
(page 100)

6 Agua Azul from the air
Seven kilometres of
waterfalls (page 102)

Gobierno is decorated with a mural by Arturo García Bustos, which depicts the state's history. The *Cathedral* (built with green serpentine stone) is Oaxaca's oldest house of worship. Compared to the other churches in the city, the interior is rather sombre.

Church of Santo Domingo
This impressive monastic church was begun in 1575 and is flanked by two large towers; the impressive façade has many niches for the numerous saints of the Dominican order. The magnificent Baroque interior overwhelms the visitor; in the words of Aldous Huxley, Santo Domingo is 'one of the most extravagantly gorgeous churches in the world'. *Daily 7 am–1 pm and 4 pm–8 pm, Alcalá/Gurrión*

MUSEUMS

Casa Benito Juárez
Benito Juárez, a full-blooded Zapotec Indian who became president of Mexico in 1858, spent some of his early years in this house of a well-to-do family. The interior gives visitors a glimpse of everyday life in the mid-19th century. *Tues–Sun 10 am–4 pm, García Vigil/Carranza*

Museo de las Culturas de Oaxaca
An absolute must: housed within the imposing walls of the former Dominican monastery are first-rate archaeological and ethnographic exhibits, including the famous gold and jade burial objects made by Mixtec goldsmiths and found in tomb no. 7 of Monte Albán. *Tues–Fri 10 am–6 pm, Sat and Sun 10 am–5 pm, to the left of the Church of Santo Domingo*

Museo Rufino Tamayo
★ The great modern painter and muralist was an admirer and a serious collector of pre-Columbian art. Before passing away, he bequeathed a large portion of his collection to the state of Oaxaca. Ironically, it is housed in five rooms of the former House of the Inquisition! The most important objects are located in the room containing pre-classical

(Olmec) finds as well as in room no. 2 (post-classical), filled with works depicting scenes of everyday life, which Tamayo used as models. *Wed–Sat 10 am–2 pm and 4 pm–7 pm, Sun 10 am–3 pm, Av. Morelos 503*

RESTAURANTS

La Casa de la Abuela
'Grandma's House' occupies the upper floor of this former manor house on the *zócalo*. A huge selection of regional dishes, sometimes accompanied by music. The restaurant is very popular, so advanced booking is strongly recommended. *Hidalgo 616, Tel. 01951/635 44, category 2*

Hostería de Alcalá
Highly recommended: efficient service, tasty food, wonderful patio. *Calle M. Alcalá, Tel. 01951/620 93, category 2*

La Olla
A combination of café, bar and restaurant offering regional fare as well as various coffees and fruit juices; small art gallery. *Reforma 402 (near Santo Domingo), Tel. 01951/666 68, category 3*

SHOPPING

Oaxaca has an outstanding reputation for its original handicrafts, many of which can be bought from Indian street vendors.

Fonart
The government-owned shop offers high-quality, reasonably priced crafts. Good for getting an idea on pricing. *Manuel N. Bravo 116*

Mercado Benito Juárez
◉ It's always market day for food and textiles near the *zócalo*; sometimes crafts are offered for sale. Very original are the wooden, handcrafted combs. *20 de Noviembre/Las Casas*

Mercado Sábado
◉ On Saturdays, a visit to this market, located in the southwestern part of the city, is recommended, when Indians offer their wares for sale. *At the second-class bus station, Periférico Oeste*

ACCOMMODATION

Camino Real
Housed in the former monastery of Santa Catalina (1576), now classified as a historical monument; one of Mexico's most exclusive addresses. *91 rooms, 5 de Mayo 300, Tel. 01951/606 11, Fax 607 32, category 1*

D'Hostel
Small hostel for young people, some private rooms; only 2 blocks away from the *zócalo*. *7 rooms, Fiallo 305, Tel. 01951/413 51, category 3*

Los Olivos
Recommended hotel with pool and (rare for Oaxaca) a large carpark. In the western part of the city, on park-like grounds. *70 rooms, Calzada F. Madero 1254, Tel. 01951/419 46, Fax 422 25, category 2*

Señorial
A colonial hotel opposite Alameda Park with (some) quiet rooms. The large patio surrounded by a gallery has been roofed and folkloric dances are per-

formed here in the evenings. *25 rooms, Portal de Flores 6 (near the zócalo), Tel. 01951/639 33, Fax 636 38, category 2*

INFORMATION

Aeroméxico
Av. Hidalgo 513, Tel. 01951/610 66

Tourist information
A list of the market days in the nearby villages is available here. *Independencia 607/García Vigil, Tel. 01951/607 17, Fax 421 36, http://oaxaca-travel.gob.mx*

SURROUNDING AREA

Mitla and El Tule (169/F4)
The first is an architectural marvel, the second a botanical sensation; both can easily be combined. Mitla is a small but unique archaeological site built mostly by the Mixtecs. The small village of 12,000 souls is only 43 km away from Oaxaca. The Palace of the Columns *(Palacio de las Columnas)* is the best preserved, replete with the unique geometrical motifs covering the walls. No figures, only the most varied geometric patterns! Almost 100,000 pieces of stone were laboriously carved and put together with marvellous precision: 'petrified weaving', in the words of Aldous Huxley. To the Indians, this was the 'place of the dead', which explains its function as a burial site; even the walls of the tombs were intricately decorated. The place was still inhabited when the Spaniards arrived in 1528. On the road to Mitla is another attraction that should not be missed: a giant cypress boasting the widest perimeter in the world, which was probably a seedling about the time of Emperor Augustus! At that time, the now arid, dusty valley was covered with forests. *El Tule*, as the tree is known throughout Mexico, dwarfs the atrium of the little village church where it stands. Indian children offer guided 'tours' to all the tourists and food and refreshment stands cluster around it. Unbelievable but true, the tree perhaps repre-

The ball court at Monte Albán, 1,000 years before the world soccer tournament

Fantastic views from the top of Monte Albán

sents the town's major source of income. *Daily 8 am–5 pm (ruins)*

Monte Albán (169/F4)

'Monte Albán is the work of men who knew their architectural business consummately well', wrote Aldous Huxley in 1932. Indeed, only 10 km away from Oaxaca is one of the most memorable sites in the whole country. Long ago, it is believed that the Olmecs started to level off the 2,000-m-high 'white mountain', as Monte Albán was known. On the 200 × 300 m area, they built temples and palaces. Scientists subdivide the complex development of the site into five stages, dating from 800 BC to 1521. The height of creativity was Monte Albán III (0–900), when the Zapotecs erected new, splendid structures, lending the site its present shape. Later, the Mixtecs converted the ceremonial centre into a burial site. One of the most interesting structures is the *Observatory* (built approx. AD 100); the structure with the pointed ground plan probably served as a place where celestial phenomena could be observed. A tunnel connects it with other buildings. As early as Monte Albán I, the *Building of the Dancers (danzantes)* was erected on the south-western side, where visitors can puzzle at the large, carved stone slabs depicting Olmec-like figures in strange positions: all are limp, naked males, and many are mutilated. They are probably not dancing, although nobody knows what they are intended to represent. *Daily 8 am–5 pm*

Yagul (169/F4)

A short trip that can be ideally added on: 15 km before Mitla is Yagul, the old religious centre of the Zapotecs and Mixtecs. Archaeologists believe it was already inhabited as early as 600 BC, but the structures seen today are from a much later time (AD 900 to 1200), from the transitional period when power passed from the Zapotecs to the Mixtecs. The site is dominated by *La Fortaleza*, a hilltop fortress. South of it are the palaces and residential areas of the former inhabitants. Endless steps connect the buildings; cacti and agaves grow everywhere. The ground plan of the *Palacio de los Seis Patios* (Palace of the Six Patios), encompassing a rectangular area of 60 × 80 m, bears witness to the skill of the master builders: the patios were built with the help of columns and giant stone blocks. *Tues–Sun 8 am–5 pm*

Zaachila (169/F4)

When famous Mexican archaeologist Alfonso Caso excavated the area in the 1940s, he had to flee for his life, so angry were the Indians, but his hunch was correct: in 1962 Roberto Gallego discovered two Zapotec tombs later taken over by the Mixtecs *(daily 10.30 am–5.30 pm)*. Only few tourists ever go to the town of Zaachila, 18 km south of Oaxaca, supposedly the last capital of the Zapotecs, yet the reliefs adorning Tomb 1 are extremely well preserved. Impressive is the representation of the 'Master of the Night' with a skull and a heart dangling in front of his chest.

The Thursday market, partly covered and with a huge selection of fruits and vegetables, is purely an Indian affair.

PALENQUE

(171/E3) ✎ Perhaps the most impressive feature of this unforgettable site is its outstanding location at the edge of the tropical rain forest, which appears almost to envelop the pyramids, temples and palaces. Apart from the magnificent setting, many of the structures are very well preserved and, decorated with many friezes, highly original. The ruins are 150 km away from Villahermosa and easily reached from there.

The town itself has 1,300 hotel beds, and the infrastructure improves with every passing year: a nice path to the ruins has been created and the old landing strip is now a regional airport; soon flights from Mérida, Cancún, Tuxtla and Oaxaca will land here. A good road to Bonampak and Yaxchilán has been completed, so that day trips to these other Mayan ruins are now possible.

Palenque acquired its present shape during the 7th century, when the priest-ruler Lord Pacal (who lived to be 80) oversaw the construction of his splendid city in AD 642. Three hundred years later, the city was mysteriously abandoned, eventually swallowed up by the encroaching jungle. As a matter of fact, we don't even know its real name: Palenque is a Spanish word meaning 'palisade' and dates back to the Dominican settlement of 1564. When Stephens visited the desolate ruins in 1840, he was very moved by 'the remains of a cultivated, polished and peculiar people wherever ... we saw evidence of their taste, their skill in the arts, their wealth and power'.

Later, in the 1880s, Alfred Maudslay, a former officer of the British foreign service, explored this and many other Mayan ruins over a period of 13 years. The result was published in five volumes in London, between 1889 and 1902, still an indispensable reference for archaeologists.

The pyramids of Palenque lie at the edge of the tropical rain forest

The site is 8 km away from the unimportant and unattractive town of the same name, whose 50,000 inhabitants cater to tourists from all over the world.

SIGHTS

Ruinas de Palenque

A sightseeing tour of the ruins should begin early, as the hot and humid climate becomes unbearable at noon. In the summer, don't forget an umbrella and insect repellent. The largest pyramid is the famous ★ Temple of the Inscriptions *(Templo de las Inscripciones)*, 21 m high, consisting of eight stone platforms layered one on top of the other. The temple on top has five entrances and 620 hieroglyphs decorate it, which explains the origin of the name.

For a long time, it was thought to be just a pyramid, until 1949 when a young Mexican archaeologist, Alberto Ruz L'Huillier, discovered a secret passageway leading to a deep crypt below the pyramid. It took him three years to clear the rubble blocking the passageway that led to the tomb of Pacal. The priest-ruler was found buried underneath an enormous, beautifully carved stone slab with all kinds of precious objects and death masks; Pacal was the Mayan equivalent of Tutankhamen! Fittingly, Ruz L'Huillier asked to be buried in Palenque. Nowadays, the restored and well-illuminated stairs lead thousands of impressed tourists to the crypt. Those who feel claustrophobic can see an excellent replica in the National Museum of Anthropology in Mexico City. ⤴ The top of the Temple affords a wonderful view of the palace *(El Palacio)*, the largest building complex restored in the 1920s by Frans Blom of Tulane University. The Palace consists of several structures built on top of a large, 100-m-long platform and grouped around four patios. The building is crowned by a 15-m-high tower *(The Observatory)*, whose top can be reached – but not recommended for those who suffer from vertigo. Throughout the complex, which included living quarters and baths, the remains of coloured stucco decoration can still be discerned. Behind the Palace, you can see parts of the underground aqueduct built by the Maya that brought water from the small River Otulum.

Beyond the river are three additional captivating structures, amongst them The Temple of the Sun, built in 692 *(Templo del Sol)* and crowned by a well-preserved roof comb *(crestería)*. The structure received its name on account of a relief of the sun that adorns the back wall of the temple.

Returning to the other side of the river, walk towards the Northern Group. These temples are built on a platform, and it is believed that they were used by merchants. The most spectacular is the Temple of the Count *(Templo del Conde)*, named after the Austrian explorer Count Frederic von Waldeck, who lived here for two years in the 1830s inside the well-preserved temple. Thanks to Waldeck's superb if rather fanciful drawings, John Lloyd Stephens was motivated to explore the region. Recently (1994), another tomb was found under Temple XIII, to the west beside the Temple of the Inscriptions. The skeleton is believed to be that of a woman, buried with her jade-mosaic death mask and jewellery *(La Reina Roja)*. Since then, excavations have intensified.

Archaeologists now believe that Palenque's central square may well be a giant necropolis. *Daily 8 am–6 pm*

MUSEUM

Museo de Palenque
The new museum is situated on the road to Palenque, filled with objects from the site. Unfortunately, the best and most important are in Mexico City. Nevertheless, there are objects made from obsidian and jade, as well as pottery and stone slabs with hieroglyphs. The models provide a good overview of the site. *2 km before reaching the site, daily 8 am–6 pm*

RESTAURANTS

Café y Arte
♱ Coffee, art and some food served amid books and magazines. *Independencia 18, Tel. 01934/507 77, category 3*

La Jaibita II
Regional seafood cuisine and Mexican dishes. In the evenings, live Mexican music. *Periférico Norte 13, Tel. 01934/510 15, category 2*

Maya
At the *zócalo*; delicious dishes. *Independencia/Hidalgo, Tel. 01934/510 96, category 3*

SHOPPING

There is only pricey kitsch in the city of Palenque. Souvenirs are also found at the entrance of the site, where some Lacandon Indians offer bows and arrows for sale.

Along the road to the ruins there are many three-star hotels. The better values are found around the *zócalo*.

Lacroix

Good location, on the *zócalo*; eight rooms surround a beautiful, quiet and green patio; informal atmosphere. *Hidalgo 8 (centre), Tel. 01934/500 14, category 3*

Maya Tulipanes

Situated in the green district of La Cañada (west of the town centre), with a large garden and very comfortable rooms. Air conditioning, pool and carpark. *36 rooms, Calle Merle Green 6 (an extension of the Hidalgo), Tel. 01934/502 01, Fax 510 04, category 2*

Plaza Palenque

A very comfortable hotel on the outskirts of the city with balconied rooms, pool and garden; a travel agency is inside. *98 rooms, Carretera a Catazajá, km 27, Tel. 01934/505 55, Fax 503 95, category 1*

INFORMATION

Tourist information

Casa de la Cultura, southern side of the zócalo, Tel. 01934/506 28, Fax 501 63, daily 9 am–5 pm

SURROUNDING AREA

Bonampak   (171/F4)

In the border region, close to Guatemala in the middle of the jungle, lies Bonampak (140 km away from Palenque). Until a few years ago, few tourists ever visited the remote ruins. Bonampak means 'painted walls' and provides the most thorough visual documentation of the Mayan civilization. The colourful murals were discovered as late as 1946 by American photographer Giles Healy, working in the Lacandon jungle on commission from the United Fruit Co. Slowly winning the confidence of the Indians, they eventually took him to their sacred temple, completely enveloped by the lush vegetation. The small city's most important structure is the *Templo de las Pinturas* (Temple of the Paintings) with realistically painted walls and ceilings depicting warriors, prisoners, sacrificial victims and musicians. They were painted to honour Chaan Muan, who ascended the throne around AD 776. The Bonampak frescoes caused archaeologists to revise their notion of the Maya as a peace-loving race; instead, autonomous city-states were engaged in constant warfare against each other.

Nowadays, Bonampak is easily reached via a good road that continues to the Río Usumacinta, where boats can be taken to Yaxchilán (60 minutes) and to Bethel in Guatemala (30 minutes). *In Palenque, some travel agencies offer combined tours of Bonampak and Yaxchilán*

Waterfalls of Agua Azul   (171/E3)

Some 65 km away from Palenque, on the road to San Cristóbal de Las Casas, a short 4-km-long road leads to the most beautiful waterfalls in the country. The 7-km-long series of light blue *(azul)* waterfalls are an unforgettable sight. Vegetation is lush but the paths leading up to the higher fall can be muddy; makeshift bridges and stone slabs lead the way to the higher falls. Walkers will find many idyllic camping spots. Modest restaurants and refreshment stands are in the park. Vehicles are allowed only on the main road. The best view of Agua Azul and Palenque, though, is from the air. Inquire at the landing strips of San Cristóbal or Palenque; four- to six-passenger planes offer ★ ↘ flights (two loops over Palenque and the waterfalls cost between US $200 and 300 for up to four passengers).

Yaxchilán   (171/F4)

This is the most important Maya site in southern Mexico apart from Palenque. A visit to this remote city in the middle of the tropical rain forest on the shores of the Río Usumacinta can easily be the highlight of the trip. The large site consists of almost 100 structures. The centre of the whole city built between AD 500 and 900 is a square containing elongated, rectangular buildings and a ball court. The friezes and sculptures are detailed and very well preserved, and represent Yaxchilán's most important works of art. Whilst the numerous stelae masterly depict the members of the ruling Jaguar Dynasty, the carved stone lintels give archaeologists a unique glimpse of the self-mutilating religious rites exercised by the Maya (for example, there is a sculpture showing a kneeling woman who passes a string with thorns through a hole in her tongue). Other magnificent originals are in the Museum of Anthropology in Mexico City and in the British Museum. All

True to their name: the waterfalls of Agua Azul

sculptures portray members of the ruling class, with their characteristic flattened foreheads and Mayan profiles. Thanks to their obsession with chronological inscriptions, a detailed list of its rulers has been compiled.

The best time to visit Yaxchilán is in the early morning hours or at dusk, when the sounds of the howling monkeys can be clearly heard for miles and tropical birds can be seen flying above the trees.

SAN CRISTÓBAL DE LAS CASAS

(171/D4) ⚊ Although this is no longer an insider's tip, the placid colonial city of 90,000 souls is still the favourite meeting spot amongst backpack tourists from all around the world and many foreign tourist groups. San Cristóbal is a good starting point for many excursions; in spite of the masses of tourists, the city has miraculously retained its original colonial-Indian charm that never fails to captivate foreigners: the large number of Indians wearing colourful costumes, the mild climate, the mostly whitewashed, single-storeyed colonial houses built with red clay bricks and forbidding wooden doors and the colonial mansions and Baroque churches. The city is named after the Dominican Bartolomé de las Casas, the tireless defender of Indian rights who became Bishop of Chiapas in 1544. San Cristóbal may be located at the 'end of the world' for some, but its atmosphere captivates most visitors.

Plaza 31 de Marzo

Numerous attractive colonial buildings border the *zócalo*, the city hall *(Palacio Municipal)* with tourist information, as well as the *Cathedral.*

The *House of the City Founder* Diego de Mazariegos, dating from the 16th century *(corner of Av. Insurgentes)*, houses an attractive hotel now; an impressive lion portal faces the Insurgentes side, the whole façade is typically Baroque. Another 16th-century structure is the *Cathedral Nuestra Señora de la Asunción,* which contains some priceless Baroque altars, rich wooden handcarved objects and paintings by Correa and Cabrera.

Church of Santo Domingo

This mid-16th-century church, with its impressive Baroque façade, is, from an art-historical point of view, the city's most important. The Habsburg double eagle is readily discernible. The interior has gold-leaf altars. *General Utrilla*

Na-Bolom Museum

This used to be the house of Frans Blom's widow, Trudi Duby-Blom, Swiss photographer and tireless defender of the Lacandon Indians. She lived here until her death in 1993. The name means *House of the Jaguar* and is now an ethnological-archaeological museum decorated with Trudi's superb portraits of the Indians. Many researchers and explorers came here for guidance before going into the Indian communities. *Tues–Sun 4.30 pm–6 pm, library (tour) 9 am–1 pm, Guerrero 33/ Comitán*

wool and cotton dyed with plant extracts. *Mon–Sat 9 am–1 pm and 4 pm–7 pm, Sun 9 am–1 pm, Av. General Utrilla 43*

RESTAURANTS

Café Colonial
Enjoy a cappuccino after a tasty meal served in a patio. *Dr. Navarro 1/Utrilla, Tel. 01967/842 99, category 3*

Casa del Pan
Unconventional, historical establishment serves vegetarian food. *Dr. Navarro 10/Domínguez, no Tel., category 3*

SHOPPING

Indian market
★ ✿ A pulsating atmosphere: Indians in their traditional costumes sell all kinds of medicinal herbs, dried fish, poultry, vegetables and fruit under a roof as well as outdoors. *Daily 7 am– 2 pm, in the northern part of the city, at the Av. Utrilla*

J'Pas Joloviletic
'Those, who weave' is the name of this cooperative of Indian women who produce and sell high-quality textiles made of

ACCOMMODATION

Posada El Paraíso
Modernized colonial house with a sunny patio, colourful and cosy; the restaurant serves delicious Swiss-Mexican food. *14 rooms, 5 de Febrero 19 (2 blocks west of the zócalo), Tel. 01967/800 85, Fax 800 81, category 2*

Rincón del Arco
A colonial house dating from 1650 with comfortably furnished rooms and an open fireplace. Reservations recommended. *32 rooms, Ejército Nacional 66, Tel. 01967/813 13, Fax 815 68, category 2*

Villa Real
An attractive, colonial-style hotel only two blocks away from the *zócalo*, with a restaurant, café and garage. Some of the rooms are rather large. The inner courtyard is a comfotable patio bordered by a pretty colonnade. *24 rooms, Juárez 8, Tel. 01967/829 30, no Fax, category 2–3*

Indian costumes

The most beautiful costumes of all are found in Chiapas, the Mexican state with the highest proportion of Indians. Every village has its own colour and pattern combinations; the women wear different *huipiles*, hand-woven sleeveless blouses decorated with brocaded or embroidered motifs. With them come a hand-woven skirt *(corte)* supported by a belt as well as a shawl *(rebozo)*. In the vicinity of San Cristóbal, the women often wear white blouses with lavishly embroidered cuffs, following an old Spanish tradition.

Tourist information

Palacio Municipal, 20 de Noviembre, Tel. 01967/807 15, Fax 806 60

Close to San Cristóbal are some very interesting, picturesque Indian towns. Most of the villagers are indifferent towards tourists, some act disapprovingly and even aggressively. Therefore, it's advisible to exercise discretion when photographing them and always to obtain their prior consent! It is not permitted to photograph the interior of a village church under any circumstances. Violation of this rule can result in a physical attack, and your camera will in any case be confiscated and you will have to pay a high fine!

Cañón del Sumidero   (171/D4)

The nearby town of Chiapa de Corzo receives many visitors because it is the starting point of adventurous boat rides in the famous Cañón del Sumidero. The journey lasts several hours, and it is particularly romantic at dusk. You see many locals waiting for customers to take them in their *lanchas*. These motor boats are intended for groups, but can also be rented by individual tourists. The boat passes by waterfalls and moss-covered rock faces as well as caves (ask to be taken to one). The greenish water is full of water lilies and dead tree trunks. The spray of the water and the airflow provide welcome relief from the heat.

Chiapa de Corzo   (171/D4)

The old colonial city of Chiapa de Corzo (founded in 1528) is situated 60 km west of San Cristóbal, and can be reached via a winding road that affords many scenic views. This city on the banks of the Río Grijalva was the very first to be founded by the Spaniards in Chiapas. In 1562, feeling homesick, they designed the *zócalo*, placing a large Moorish-style fountain with high arches vaguely resembling the Spanish royal crown in the middle of it. The city boasts a lively *plaza* and some attractive colonial buildings, but Chiapa de Corzo is best known for its enormous choice of exquisite lacquerwork, the country's best. A museum is even devoted to the art of lacquer: the *Museo de Laca (daily 9 am–7 pm)* on the *zócalo*, which documents the infinite colours and patterns employed by the craftsmen.

Rustic, small restaurants offering local cuisine group around the boat ramps. For a highly recommended and comfortable overnight stay: *La Ceiba (42 rooms, Av. Domingo Ruiz 300, Tel. 01961/603 89, Fax 607 73, category 3).*

San Juan Chamula   (171/D4)

★ The most frequently visited Indian village in Chiapas is San Juan Chamula (about 10 km to the north-west), the religious centre of the Chamula Indians. The Indians tolerate tourists because they are a source of income, but it is necessary to pay a fee to walk around and photograph the town (but neither the people nor the interior of the fascinating village church). An

Colourful Indian costumes are characteristic of many villages in Chiapas

Indian carrying a big stick accompanies every visitor and sees to it that regulations are obeyed. It is quite an experience to see the candle-lit, incense-filled church interior covered by pine needles and to witness the Indians kneel in front of their saints, drink Coca-Cola, light candles, sing, pray and carry on animated conversations with each other.

Tenejapa (171/D4)
An unpaved road through the beautiful highlands takes visitors to this village only 30 km away, but the journey takes two hours. The community of Tzetzal Indians lies in a basin surrounded by mountains and is well known for the high-quality textiles produced by the weaving cooperative. The many different belts and blankets are offered for sale throughout the week, but the largest selection is on Sunday, the local market day. A small museum displays village crafts and a modest guest house offers overnight accommodation.

Zinacantán (171/D4)
This little village, only 10 km north-west of San Cristóbal, is inhabited by Tzotzil Indians. Many buses go to the 'Place of Bats'. The typical cobbled streets are very picturesque, but do keep in mind that it is prohibited to photograph anything here! The interior of the *village church* bears witness to the syncretism of Indian beliefs and Catholic faith. It is traditional for the bachelors of this village to wear flower-embroidered, pink ponchos decorated with tassels.

Oil and Olmecs

*In the insalubrious swamps, islands and lagoons,
the oldest culture of the Americas was born*

The coast of the Gulf of Mexico stands for a hot, tropical and very humid, enervating climate coupled with a largely primitive infrastructure. Pretty, unspoilt beaches are few and far between, scattered along the long, swampy Gulf coast, a mosquito paradise if there ever was one. In spite of these formidable obstacles, the very first civilization of the New World was born here and it was also here on the Gulf Coast that Cortés and his band of adventurers landed in 1519, very close to modern-day Veracruz. Not a single *plaza* in Mexico is more lively, more Caribbean than this one. In the vicinity, old pre-Columbian ceremonial centres are juxtaposed with oil refineries. Indeed, it was the search for the black gold that led to the discovery of the lost cities of the mysterious culture of the Olmecs, known by posterity mostly for their gigantic carved stone heads.

VERACRUZ

(167/F5) Mexico's marine gate to the outside world is the tropical, Caribbean-influenced harbour of Veracruz, the country's largest. It is no coincidence that you'll hear

*Restored Art Nouveau buildings
characterize the Zona Luz in
Villahermosa*

many children whistling the catchy tune 'La Bamba', which after all was born here. The city's 800,000 inhabitants have a reputation for being easy-going and open; doubtless this exciting place is unique in Mexico: Baroque buildings, Spanish *plazas* bordered by graceful palms, and in the streets people from all over the world. The attractive *zócalo* is the favourite meeting place amongst sailors and couples, who listen to the soft sounds of the marimba. During Carnival, no other city celebrates more joyfully and boisterously than this one.

SIGHTS

Castillo de San Juan de Ulúa
During colonial times, Veracruz was the place where all the gold and silver bound for Europe left the shores – no wonder that the surrounding coast was full of pirates. Therefore the Spaniards erected a massive fortress on a coral island directly in front of the harbour. San Juan de Ulúa has been the scene of numerous battles and over the years has been taken by the French and the Americans (in 1847 during the Mexican-American War and in 1914 during the Mexican Revolution). Political prisoners, such as Benito Juárez, once filled its infamous dungeons. More recently, it has been used as a backdrop for

MARCO POLO SELECTION: THE GULF OF MEXICO

1 Plaza de Armas in Veracruz
This is the birthplace of the world hit 'La Bamba' (page 110)

2 El Tajín
The builders of the mysterious and unique Pyramid of the Niches are unknown (page 112)

3 Parque La Venta
A tropical park in modern Villahermosa planned by a poet and decorated with some very unusual monuments: the stony monumental heads of the mysterious Olmecs, discovered only 60 years ago (page 113)

Hollywood films, such as *Romancing the Stone*. *Daily 10 am–5 pm, over the dyke (continuation of the Av. Ulúa), by ferry from the Malecón, or take the bus from the Plaza de la República*

Plaza de Armas
★ This city square, also known as *Plaza de la Constitución*, can be regarded as the city's giant 'living room'. With a tropical atmosphere, it is bordered by majestic buildings and adorned with palms and lush colourful vegetation. Under the arcades *(portales)*, one can sit for hours sipping the famous coffee (the state of Veracruz is the largest producer) in the traditional cafés, listening to the sound of the marimba, a xylophone-like instrument introduced by the black slaves. The city hall *(Palacio Municipal)*, which has an attractive patio, dates from the 17th century and the cathedral *(La Parroquia)*, a splendid structure, was completed in 1734; both abut the *plaza*.

Plaza de la República
The narrow, long square is lined with public buildings, mostly from the 19th century: the customs house *(Aduana Marítima)*, main post office *(Correos y Telégrafos)* with a typically elaborate façade and the ornately adorned train station *(Estación de Ferrocarriles)* full of tiles are worth a look. The biggest building lies on the western side of the square, the *Registro Civil*, the country's first registry. *Opposite the harbour*

MUSEUMS

Acuario de Veracruz
◈ The city aquarium is one of the nation's best. In its 100 pools, visitors can admire the underwater fauna of the Gulf Coast. *Daily 10 am–7 pm, Bulevar Camacho, Playón de Hornos*

Museo de la Ciudad
The city's most important museum, it has a good collection of Olmec artefacts in addition to other archaeological finds from the Totonac and Huaxtec cultures; interesting is a documentation of the colonial era of Veracruz. *Tues–Sun 10 am–6 pm, Zaragoza 397*

RESTAURANTS

Many restaurants have numerous tables outside where fish and shellfish are grilled and served.

Malecón del Paseo and along the *Bulevar Ávila Camacho.*

El Gaucho

Breakfast a la veracruzana; at midday and in the evening, Argentinian-style steaks and pasta dishes are served. The regional fish dishes are also recommended. *Bernal Díaz del Castillo 187/Colón, Tel. 0129/35 04 11, category 2*

La Gran Cantina

A restaurant and bar with a lot of business; the speciality is Mexican paella. *Bulevar Ávila Camacho 2681, Tel. 0129/35 07 65, category 2*

ACCOMMODATION

Central

Modest hotel but good service; mostly local guests. *22 rooms, Díaz Mirón 1612, Tel. 0129/37 22 22, Fax 37 23 50, category 3*

Imperial

Stylish colonial house in the city centre, loud and lively. *81 rooms, Miguel Lerdo 153, Tel./Fax 0129/32 87 88, category 2*

Mocambo

This old hotel has the same name as the beach and is 8 km away from the city; Moorish-colonial luxury amid a large and luxuriant garden. *132 rooms, Calzada Ruíz Cortines 4000, Tel. 0129/22 02 01, Fax 22 02 12, category 1*

INFORMATION

Tourist information

Palacio Municipal, Zócalo, Tel. 9129/32 19 99, Fax 31 25 43, www.veracruz-turismo.gob.mx

SURROUNDING AREA

La Antigua   (167/F4–5)

This small fishing village is easily reached via the good, paved road MEX 180 and marks the spot where Cortés landed almost 500 years ago. The *House of Hernán Cortés* has been virtually swallowed up by the giant tropical trees. The heavy, muggy air drains all your energy. A small, white *chapel* is said to be the first Christian structure on Mexican soil.

Jalapa   (167/E4)

Lying at an altitude of 1,400 m and 130 km north-west of Veracruz, the state capital is surrounded by lush vegetation and coffee plantations. It is also known as Xalapa, pronounced

The roots of ancient tropical trees are enveloping the Casa de Cortés in La Antigua

the same way. This college town has 350,000 inhabitants, and its most important attraction is the *Museo de Antropología (Tues–Sun 9 am–5 pm, Av. Xalapa),* the most important archeological museum in Mexico after that in Mexico City. The first-rate displays show the most important finds of the Olmec culture (especially the monumental heads) as well as those of the Totonacs and the Huaxtecs, the three 'Gulf Cultures'.

El Tajín (167/E3)
★ 240 km north-west of Veracruz lies a mysterious pre-Columbian site whose heyday was between AD 300 and 1100. Some of the structures and temples, especially the 25-m-high Pyramid of the Niches *(Pirámide de los Nichos)* – the only one in Mexico – were built in the 7th century. The seven-storeyed structure contains 364 niches, which added to the temple on top give us the number of days it takes for the earth to orbit the sun. It is assumed that the Totonacs built it (El Tajín is in Totonac country), but it has not been proved. Only about one-tenth of it has been excavated, including several ball courts. By the entrance, there is a modest *museum,* then comes the excavated and totally restored part called *Tajín Grande*, with the Pyramid of the Niches and the southern ball court *(Juego de Pelota Sur)*. Here, one can easily discern the pre-Columbian masters being depicted in the stone reliefs. Archaeologists believe that the game had ritualistic and religious significance, and in many cases the losers paid with their lives. About 1 km farther on is the other, mostly unexcavated part called *Tajín Chico*, still covered by grass, including the truly enormous Building of the Columns *(Edificio de las Columnas)*.

VILLAHERMOSA

(171/D2) Tabasco is small in size but big in natural resources. Its capital city, Villahermosa (beautiful village), was founded in 1598 on the banks of the mighty Río Grijalva. Its 350,000 inhabitants are well-off by Mexican standards; agriculture and oil generated the wealth. For many decades, the city barely grew owing to the insalubrious climate and the large swamps and jungle surrounding it. The face of the city has now been transformed by oil, and modern skyscrapers as well as beautifully restored colonial buildings characterize the state capital.

SIGHTS

Zona Luz
The colonial city centre was completely remodelled and many of the Spanish manor houses were painstakingly restored, and Art Nouveau street lamps added. Now, many nice restaurants, cafés and shops line the streets.

MUSEUMS

CICOM
The Centro de Investigación de las Culturas Olmeca y Maya is an important destination for archaeologists. Dozens of specialists come here to unravel mysteries of the Olmec and Mayan cultures. They built the four-storeyed *Museo Regional de Antropología Carlos Pellicer Cámara*, which houses one of the most famous of all pre-Columbian collections. *Daily*

9 am–8 pm, Av. Carlos Pellicer 511 (on the river bank)

Parque Museo La Venta

★ In 1938, the year Mexico's oil was nationalized, workers drilling near the jungle community of La Venta, 130 km east of the state capital, made an astonishing discovery: they unearthed a colossal 3,000-year-old basalt face. The most amazing thing was that there were no stones of that size anywhere near the site, which only deepened the mystery. Sooner or later, more of these colossal, 25-tonne-heads came to light and little by little, archaeologists (especially American) have been piecing together the history of the people who carved these enormous basalt blocks and gave them their eyes, thick lips and wide noses. All have slightly different facial features, thus it is believed that they represent famous warriors or kings. Owing to the perennially hot and humid climate, no written documents of any kind have survived. What is truly remarkable is that they somehow transported the huge boulders from the distant volcanic Sierra de Los Tuxtlas to their cities. Nowadays, you can admire 33 of these unique works of art in a first-rate, open-air museum created expressly for that purpose by Carlos Pellicer. A zoo with an aviary has recently been added to the complex, and an attractive restaurant lures the visitor. *Daily 8 am–5 pm, Av. A. Ruíz Cortínes*

RESTAURANTS

In the *Zona Luz,* Villahermosa's historic city centre, restaurants abound. Try the local speciality found in the menus, the *pejelagarto* (a fresh-water fish prepared in a variety of ways). In the evening, take a river tour with the restaurant-boat *Capitán Beulo (at the Madrazo dock).*

Karukay

Japanese cuisine. The speciality is sushi. *Lamberto Castellanos 302, Tel. 0193/14 42 41, category 2*

La Paella

Traditional Spanish cuisine; the speciality is paella with shellfish. *Paseo Usumacinta 410, Tel. 0193/ 15 25 53, category 3*

Los Tulipanes

Good regional dishes as well as fish and shellfish from the Gulf of Mexico. *On the grounds of the CI-COM, Tel. 0193/12 92 09, category 2*

ACCOMMODATION

Holiday Inn Villahermosa Plaza

A modern hotel in the district of Tabasco 2000; surrounded by greenery. *222 rooms, Prolongación Paseo Tabasco 1407, Tel. 0193/15 44 00, Fax 16 45 69, category 1*

Plaza Independencia

Comfortable and centrally located – and highly recommended. *89 rooms, Independencia 123, Tel. 0193/ 12 12 99, Fax 14 47 24, category 2*

Tabasco

In the Zona Luz. Not particularly attractive, but reasonably priced. *31 rooms, Lerdo 317/Juárez, Tel. 0193/12 00 77, no Fax, category 3*

INFORMATION

Tourist information

Lerdo 101, Tel. 0193/15 06 93, Fax 16 28 90

Pyramids and palm trees

Endless tropical beaches of Mexico's Caribbean coastline lure the visitor while imposing Mayan ruins provide a dramatic backdrop

The Yucatán Peninsula resembles a huge, flat disk, which separates the Gulf of Mexico from the Caribbean Sea. Most tourists flock to the eastern Caribbean coast, as it is here that a perfectly intact holiday infrastructure awaits them. Indeed, in the internationally famous holiday strongholds of Cancún and Cozumel, the season is always perfect: it's always warm and the sun is always shining on the fine, white and powdery beaches with turquoise to emerald-green, inviting waters at a temperature of at least 25°C (77°F).

Underwater sports enthusiasts find a unique paradise in the waters of this beautiful sea, where giant sea turtles and multitudes of colourful tropical fish swim. On Cozumel's south-west coast, the Palancar coral reef with its wonderful reef gardens, caves and steep rock walls waits for divers to discover it. And as if that were not enough, only a stone's throne away from the coast and the holiday resorts, some of the continent's most impressive and best preserved pre-Columbian ruins can be reached in a few hours.

Not only is the wonderfully restored, world-renowned archaeological site of Chichén Itzá, possibly the largest and most frequented in Mexico, situated in Yucatán, but there are also a great number of very interesting, though less spectacular Mayan cities here, such as the fortified Tulum built atop high cliffs overlooking the sea, or the mysterious Cobá set deep within the thick, tropical jungle.

Yucatán is the land of the Maya. Nowadays, all over this large peninsula you will see the descendants of the great master builders and astronomers. Women wear light, white dresses with colourful embroidery at the yoke, which, in view of the hot and humid climate prevailing throughout most of the year, is certainly the most sensible way to dress.

The Toltec-inspired 'Chac-Mool' figures are common throughout Yucatán

CAMPECHE

(**172/B3**) The capital (pop. 250,000) of the state bearing the same name is the oldest Spanish city on the peninsula. Francisco Montejo, the conqueror of Yucatán, founded it in 1540. Owing to the constant raids of English and Dutch pirates, it was decided early on to fortify the city with imposing ramparts *(baluartes)*, whose remains can still be seen. Most visitors come to Campeche from Mérida, the peninsula's largest city, only a two-hour drive away thanks to the well-built, paved road MEX 180. If you are interested in visiting the archaeological sites of the state, take the slower but more interesting country road.

SIGHTS

Baluartes (ramparts)
It is possible to walk on the remains of the 2.5-km-long defensive wall that once surrounded the entire colonial city, interrupted here and there by massive ramparts. Many of the fascinating historical buildings can be visited as well; for example, in the old *ramparts of Santa Rosa* and *San Juan*, facing away from the sea, are the Tourist Information Office and the folkloric ballet, whilst the grounds of the (partly destroyed) *Baluarte de Santiago* (Calle 8 north of the city centre) has been converted into the *Botanical Gardens of Xmuch Haltún.*

Casa de la Cultura
The colonial wealth of the city can readily be seen in its present cultural centre, which is housed in a former, splendidly restored Spanish manor house. The Moorish façade is covered with beautiful, hand-made tiles. Exhibitions, art and folklore. *Plaza Principal (southern side)*

Catedral
The oldest church in Yucatán was built in 1540 and boasts two massive towers, which make it an easily identifiable structure. *Plaza Principal*

Mansión Carvajal
Magnificent colonial house graced with an impressive façade, Moorish arches and wrought-iron. *Plaza Principal (northern side)*

MUSEUMS

Museo Arqueológico
An important part of the archaeological finds from southern Yucatán is exhibited inside the old fortress; in addition: exhibits documenting the history of sea navigation and piracy. *Tues–Sun 9 am–5 pm, Baluarte de la Soledad, Zócalo*

Museo de Historia
Pre-Columbian finds, fortress models, arms. *Tues–Sat 9 am–7 pm, Sun 9 am–1 pm, Baluarte San Carlos, Plaza Moch Cuouh/Ruíz Cortines*

RESTAURANTS

Marganzo
Regional cuisine; specializing in seafood. *Calle 8 No. 261 (between Calles 59 and 57), Tel. 01981/138 98, category 2*

La Parroquia
♣ Open around the clock, this is a popular meeting place for young people who flock here to savour 'home-made' dishes. *Calle 55 No. 8 (between Calles 10 and 12), Tel. 01981/625 30, category 3*

SHOPPING

An arts-and-crafts centre has been opened in the Baluarte San Car-

MARCO POLO SELECTION: YUCATÁN

1 Mérida
A colonial city with charm and atmosphere (page 124)

2 Uxmal
The Pyramid of the Magician consists of five temples (page 131)

3 Cobá
Walk early in the morning through the jungle and climb to the peninsula's highest pyramid (page 135)

4 Cozumel
Snorkelling amid colourful Caribbean fish (page 122)

5 Breakfast with history
On the roof terrace of the museum in Cozumel (page 121)

los; here you'll find a very good selection of panama hats. *Calle 8*

ACCOMMODATION

América
Although this former stylish hotel has seen better days, it is good and moderately priced; the American manager is friendly and ready to help. *52 rooms, Calle 10 No. 252 (in the city centre), Tel. 01981/645 88, Fax 105 56, category 3*

Baluartes
A modern hotel separated from the sea by the seaside road; comfortable accommodation. *100 rooms, Av. 16 de Septiembre 128 (city centre), Tel. 01981/639 11, Fax 624 10, category 2*

Colonial
This colonial manor house was the residence of a Spanish lieutenant and his wife during the Spanish period; it has been a hotel for 50 years. *30 rooms, Calle 14 No. 122 (between Calles 55 and 57), Tel. 01981/622 22, Fax 626 30, category 3*

INFORMATION

Tourist information
Calle 12 No. 153 (between Calles 53 and 55), Tel. 01981/655 93, Fax 667 67

SURROUNDING AREA

Edzná (172/B3)
This important Mayan site is situated approx. 50 km south-east of Campeche. Edzná experienced its heyday between AD 600 and 900, but archaeologists believe it was founded eight centuries earlier. Maya experts think the city once had 60,000 inhabitants, and like so many Maya cities it entered a period of mysterious, marked decline after AD 800.

Nowadays, the central *plaza* (150 × 100 m) is surrounded by several restored structures; the sandstone temples are still partly decorated with the old stucco masks. A *ball court*, an *amphitheatre* and an extended *canal system* have been excavated. The 30-m-high, five-storeyed pyramid is called *Pirámide de los Cinco Pisos* and towers above the entire site; it can be seen from afar.

CANCÚN

(173/F1) For those who love vast, white beaches, gourmet restaurants and a wide selection of water sports, Cancún is the ideal place (pop. 400,000). Situated on a 25-km-long, L-shaped sandbank between the Caribbean Sea and the more than 100 square metre Nichupté Lagoon, it boasts more than two dozen very comfortable hotels.

Everybody swims, surfs, snorkels, visits the Pok-ta-Poko or the Caesar Park golf course or strolls leisurely in one of the luxurious shopping centres. Cancún's exclusive Caribbean atmosphere continues to lure more and more tourists away from Acapulco. Although the country's 'youngest city' – unlike 'Old Aca' – has no friendly, cosy city centre with a *zócalo*, it is nevertheless cleaner and offers better overall service. The new pedestrian precincts in Cancún's city centre, around the main street, Avenida Tulum, encompasses more than 100 shops, boutiques, restaurants and discos. For those who are not fully satisfied with sand and shopping, the magnificent pre-Columbian ruins, charming colonial towns and nature reserves beckon. Organized bus tours to Chichén Itzá and Tulum are offered in all hotels, some even offer tours to more remote places, such as Cobá. Every hour, a comfortable luxury bus leaves Cancún towards the south, following the coastal highway that takes visitors to Xcaret and Sian Ka'an, amongst other destinations. Even the monastery and pyramids of Izamal can be reached in only one day.

MUSEUM

Museo de Antropología

This small museum has exhibits dealing with Mexican history. A visit before going to the archaeological sites is strongly recommended, as the many models give a good overview of the ruins; at around 6 pm, the Ballet Folklórico gives a show. *Tues–Sat 10 am–2 pm and 5 pm–8 pm, Convention Center*

RESTAURANTS

100% Natural

⚘ A real alternative cuisine: many vegetables, fruits and freshly pressed juices; jazz is played every evening. *Sunyaxchén 62, Tel. 0198/ 84 36 17, category 3*

Gipsy's

The breakfast buffet can be had as early as 7 am; lobster is served at noon. For the little ones, there is an aquarium. In the evenings, flamenco dancing. Good view of the lagoon. *Paseo Kukulcán, km 11 (opposite Continental Villas), Tel. 0198/83 21 20, category 2*

Lorenzillos

⚞ Number one in the hotel zone: delicious fish dishes are served inside a huge, thatched, tropical-style cottage with a very romantic view of the lagoon. *Paseo Kukulcán, km 11 (opposite Hotel Continental Villas), Tel. 0198/83 12 54, category 1*

OK Maguey

People meet for breakfast starting at 8 am; there is lobster in the evenings. In between, you can eat all you can afford to. *Plaza Kukulcán (Paseo Kukulcán, km 13), Tel. 0198/85 05 03, category 2*

Pericos

Lively restaurant in the city centre where marimbas and *mariachis* can always be heard; Mexican cuisine. *Av. Yaxchilán 61, Tel. 0198/84 31 52, category 2*

SHOPPING

✝ The ultramodern shopping centre *Plaza Caracol* at the *Paseo Kukulcán* in the hotel zone offers just about everything under the sun. Apart from designer's clothes, local arts and crafts can also be found *(Galerías Colonial, Las Mañanitas)* and, last but not least, well-stocked bookshops. A wide selection of modern and Mexican clothes can be bought at *María Bonita* in the *Costa Blanca shopping centre* beside the Plaza Caracol. Numerous small shops are located along *Av. Tulum.*

ACCOMMODATION

The price of accommodation in Cancún is significantly higher than in other parts of Mexico. The modern, luxurious beach hotels are filled with holidaymakers who have booked packaged tours, so the better values can be found in the city centre and around Av. Yaxchilán.

Continental Villas Plaza

Lively, large facility situated on the beach, offering a wide animation programme. A particularly beautiful restaurant is located on the beach. *638 rooms, Paseo Kukulcán, km 11.5, Tel. 0198/ 81 55 00, Fax 81 56 94, category 1*

Fiesta Americana Condesa

An architecturally interesting beach holiday resort with two curved pools and lush tropical vegetation. *476 rooms, Paseo Kukulcán, km 16.5, Tel. 0198/85 10 00, Fax 85 18 00, category 1*

Holiday Inn Express

The balcony rooms surround the two pools (one for children). Nice patio garden, but the hotel lacks a restaurant and is far from the beach. *120 rooms, Paseo Pok-ta-*

In the mood for luxury? Then visit Fiesta Americana on the beach at Cancún

Pok, Tel. 0198/83 22 00, Fax 83 25 10, category 2

Youth hostel CREA

🕈 An ultramodern building right on the beach. *550 beds, Paseo Kukulcán, km 3.2, Tel. 0198/83 13 37, category 3*

SPORTS & LEISURE

Almost two dozen marinas offer deep-sea fishing, water skiing, sailing and diving.

Aqua World

Submarine trips and various other water sports. *Paseo Kukulcán, km 15.2, Tel. 0198/85 22 88*

Rancho Loma Bonita

Horseback riding on the beach and into the jungle. *MEX 307 between Puerto Morelos and Playa del Carmen, Tel. 0198/ 87 54 65*

INFORMATION

Aeroméxico

Av. Cobá 80, Tel. 0198/86 01 23

Tourist information

Av. Tulum 10, Tel. 0198/87 42 42, Fax 84 04 37, www.cancun.com

COZUMEL

(173/F2) Long before it ever became a tourist magnet, this small island was one of the preferred haunts of Dutch, French and particularly English pirates, amongst them Wallace, who sailed from here to found the colony of Belize. Much later, in the 1960s, world-famous diver and underwater cameraman Jacques Cousteau was so fascinated by the underwater sights of this small Caribbean island (45 × 15 km, pop. 65,000 inhabitants) that he filmed a documentary, thereby putting it on the map. Over the years, the trickle of tourists soon became a flood. Most of them come here more for diving than anything else, the Palancar coral reef being the preferred destination, but also to the underwater caves and the Chankanaab Lagoon well known for their tropical flora and fauna. Even beginners can admire the

A Caribbean dream come true: the inviting tropical beach of Cozumel

120

underwater attractions; many diving schools offer lessons and diving tours are also given. Large cruise ships moor at the island on a regular basis, and since Cozumel is a duty-free zone, the businesses teem with shoppers from all corners of the world. Connections to the mainland are excellent thanks to two airlines and several ferryboats (from Playa del Carmen). The island's main hub and largest city is San Miguel de Cozumel, situated on the west coast.

SIGHTS

There are several pre-Columbian sites scattered across the island, but they are small and have hardly been excavated. A visit to them is recommended only for those with a profound knowledge of archaeology, for example to the *Mayan ruins of El Cedral,* 3 km east of the San Francisco beach, or to *San Gervasio* in the northern part of the island. Tours to the much more important ruins of the peninsula are offered by many of the island's travel agencies.

Chankanaab Lagoon
A nature reserve has been created around this tropical lagoon. The crystal-clear water is the home of countless tropical fish of all sizes and gaudy colours, which swim placidly in front of admiring snorkellers. An attractive, open-air restaurant is located on the spot. *About 9 km south of San Miguel*

MUSEUM

Museo de la Isla de Cozumel
This modern museum, built in the 1980s displays archaeological objects and other items found

underwater. It is within walking distance of the mooring. A popular ★ restaurant with open-air tables is located upstairs. *(category 3). Daily 10 am–6 pm, Av. Melgar/Calle 6*

RESTAURANTS

Carlos 'n' Charlies
⚑ Mexican cuisine inside a pub, popular amongst young people; rock and jazz for dancing on the roof garden. *Av. Melgar 11, Tel. 01987/201 91, category 2*

Costa Brava
A huge selection of fish dishes, clams and all kinds of seafood. Already full for breakfast at 7 am. *Av. Melgar 599, Tel. 01987/251 26, category 2*

La Laguna
Fish and seafood specialities are especially tasty in the atmosphere of this palm-thatched cottage directly on the beach. Open only from 10.30 am to 4.30 pm! *Chankanaab National Park, category 2*

Las Palmeras
⚑ Already at 7 am, backpackers from all over the world meet here for breakfast to discuss their plans. *Av. Melgar (Plaza Central), Tel. 01987/238 83, category 3*

SHOPPING

Los Cinco Soles
From the patio-restaurant appropriately called *Pancho's* (built to resemble an hacienda), you can walk to the shops where high-quality, original Mexican crafts are offered for sale. *Av. Melgar Norte 27/Calle 8*

The expensive hotels are all on the west coast, directly on the beach. Cheaper accommodation can be found in San Miguel, although even here the prices are higher than average. During the high season, modestly priced rooms are hard to find.

Casa del Mar

A modern beach resort in the Zona Hotelera Sur. *106 rooms, Costera Sur, km 4, Tel. 01987/216 65, Fax 218 55, category 2*

Pepita

⚚ Eduardo Ruiz runs the place with a lot of enthusiasm. *35 rooms, Av. 15 Sur 120, Tel. 01987/200 98, Fax 202 01, category 3*

Sol Caribe

An impressive lobby built in the tropical cottage (palapa) style, with a lot of marble and a huge, lagoon-shaped pool. A tunnel beneath the street leads to the beach. *322 rooms, Playa Paraíso, about 3 km south of San Miguel, Tel. 01987/207 00, Fax 213 01, category 1*

SPORTS & BEACHES

Beaches

There are many lovely, some even empty, beaches in Cozumel; the most popular are *San Francisco* (about 17 km south of San Miguel) and *San Juan* (2 km to the north). The purists prefer the empty beach of *Palancar* (approx. 19 km to the south and reached only by a path).

Diving

★ Numerous glass-bottom boats give the first-time visitor a good idea of the underwater marvels of the island. Almost one-half of Cozumel's visitors, though, prefer to experience these marvels first hand by diving into the clear, warm Caribbean waters. For this reason, many diving clubs rent diving equipment and offer lessons. However, beginners should exercise caution.

INFORMATION

Tourist information

Plaza Central, Tel. 01987/209 72, and in the museum

ISLA MUJERES

(173/F1) Eleven kilometres offshore, north of Cancún, lies the tiny, 8-km-long and up to 900-m-wide 'Island of Women'. The main attractions of this Caribbean holiday destination are the famous diving spots, praised by those who prefer a more tranquil atmosphere. This island of 15,000 souls is not only a more quiet destination than neighbouring Cozumel, but also more moderately priced, so it generally attracts a younger crowd. The island has a small airfield, but most of the visitors arrive by ferry from Punta Sam or Puerto Juárez. During pre-Columbian times, the uninhabited island served as a place of pilgrimage. The first European to land here, in 1517, was Francisco Fernández de Córdoba and his crew, who found clay figures representing only women, thus giving the island its name.

SIGHTS

Cueva de los Tiburones Dormidos

More experienced divers visit this cave in the *northern part of the island* where real sleeping sharks can be seen, the only place in the world.

El Garrafón

This marine national park situated in the south-western corner of the island is a favourite destination. Many fish and marine organisms swim about; diving masks and flippers for rent. Restaurant and snack bar. *Daily, 8 am–5 pm*

Hacienda Mundaca

Very close to El Garrafón lie the remains of the former hacienda of the pirate Fermín Mundaca. According to legend, the buccaneer fell in love with an island beauty and in order to please her, built this pompous structure, hoping she would then marry him. Although his love remained unrequited, he still decided to spend his final years here.

Ix Chel temple

⚜ This 10th-century Mayan temple, built in honour of the goddess of fertility Ix Chel, is situated in one of the island's best locations, on top of south-facing cliffs, directly above the sea. Fantastic views. *Reached by a footpath from the lighthouse.*

RESTAURANTS

The island's restaurants are found mostly in the 'capital' in the north, amongst which are many beach restaurants. The most attractive one is in the Na Balam hotel: tranquillity and smooth, white Caribbean sand.

El Nopalito

This is the meeting place of those who appreciate Mexican-inspired health-food cuisine. The café-restaurant also functions as a place to exchange information and make contacts. *Guerrero 70/Matamoros, Tel. 01987/705 55, category 3*

SHOPPING

Artesanías El Nopal

High-quality Mexican arts and crafts, such as woven articles, embroidery, wooden objects, ceramics, jewellery. *Guerrero/Matamoros*

ACCOMMODATION

Within walking distance of the ferry mooring are several modestly priced, category-3 hostels and small hotels. Three recommended ones are:

Francis Arlene

In the town centre, yet quiet, built in the colonial style with a patio. All rooms have terraces; highly recommended. *22 rooms, Av. Guerrero 7, Tel./Fax 01987/703 10, category 3*

Na Balam

Situated on the beach, away from the others. Boat tours offered; water sports, fishing. *31 rooms, Zazil Ha 118 (Playa Norte), Tel. 01987/702 79, Fax 704 46, category 1*

Posada del Mar

Rooms with balconies overlooking the ocean at the beach. A large, park-like garden, a big pool area with a lot of greenery, with a nearby aqueduct and a waterfall. Centrally located, but not on the main street. Highly recommended. *46 rooms, Av. Rueda Medina 15A, Tel. 01987/703 00, Fax 702 66, www.mexicoweb.com/travel/posada.html, category 2*

Tourist information

Palacio Municipal, Hidalgo/Morelos, Tel. 01987/700 98, Fax 703 16, www.mundacatravel.com/islamujeres

MÉRIDA

(172/C2) ★ The former colonial city (pop. 1.3 million) is very popular owing to its exhilarating atmosphere. The city has many attractive ⚑ squares where the young people congregate; the beautiful, tree-lined ⚑ Paseo de Montejo, a magnificent boulevard inaugurated in 1906, is Mérida's answer to the Champs Elysées. The large, French-style mansions on both sides were built during the sisal boom in the early 1900s. In the many clothing shops, women can buy (and wear) the *huipil*, a white blouse with colourful embroidery, ideal attire for the hot climate; men can purchase the typical *guayabera*, a large shirt with many front pockets.

Mérida, founded in 1542, is still the largest metropolis on the peninsula, and wasn't connected to the rest of Mexico until 1950. Therefore, it is still quite different from other cities and has managed to retain its unique atmosphere.

Casa de Montejo

Many consider this large manor house, built in 1549 by conquistador and city founder Francisco de Montejo, to be the most beautiful colonial residence in the country. It is now a bank, yet parts of it can be visited. Very beautiful is the Plateresque façade with the Montejo family seal and the large, light-flooded patios. *Southern side of the zócalo*

Catedral

The foundations of this large Baroque church were laid back in 1561 and the stones of a Mayan pyramid that occupied the same spot were used to construct it (a common practice then). The chapel in the interior of this church (one of Mexico's oldest) has an interesting wooden sculpture called 'Cristo de las Ampollas' (Christ of the Blisters). *Eastern side of the zócalo*

Palacio de Gobierno

〰 In the ballroom of this government building, there are several impressive paintings by Fernando Castro Pacheco. The balcony upstairs is an ideal spot for photographers wanting to get the perfect snapshot of the cathedral and the *zócalo*. *Northern side of the zócalo*

Palacio Municipal

An old building full of history: on 15 September 1821, the independence of the Yucatán Peninsula was proclaimed from this building, which is easily recognizable owing to its high clocktower dating from 1735. Behind it lies the *Jardín del Componista*. *Western side of the zócalo*

Museo de Antropología

The museum housed in the Palacio Cantón displays Mayan and other pre-Columbian artefacts. Especially interesting are the sacrificial offerings dredged from the depths of the Holy Cenote in Chichén Itzá. *Tues–Sat 9 am–8 pm, Sun 8 am–2 pm, Paseo Montejo/Calle 43*

Museo de Arte Popular

This small, yet interesting, folklore museum gives a very good overview of costumes as well as arts and crafts. Those who are thinking of purchasing typical products made in Mérida should visit this museum first in order to learn about their manufacture. *Tues–Sat 9 am–6 pm, Sun 9 am–2 pm, Calle 59 No. 441/ Calle 50*

RESTAURANTS

Alberto's Continental

A house dating from colonial times with Cuban tiles and the remains of walls from ruined temples. International and Lebanese cuisine; one of the city's finest culinary addresses. *Calle 64 No. 482/ Calle 57, Tel. 0199/28 53 67, category 1*

Los Almendros

A very wide selection of Yucatecan specialities, such as *cochinita pibil*, pork baked in banana leaves and prepared with the red seeds of the *achiote*; very spicy and heavy. *Calle 50 No. 493/Plaza de la Mejorada, Tel. 0199/28 54 59, category 2*

Carlos 'n' Charlie's

⚓ Seafood and American food; fast and efficient service; children are welcome. *Paseo Montejo 447N, Tel. 0199/26 02 74, category 2*

La Casona

Elegant dining atmosphere inside a Patrician home. Italian and

local cuisine, seafood specialities. *Calle 60 No. 434, Tel. 0199/ 23 83 48, category 1*

SHOPPING

Lucy Curios

All kinds of arts and crafts, some very original; ponchos, shoes made of sisal and the typical *guayaberas. Bazar de Artesanías Lucas de Gálvez, Calle 56/ Calle 67*

El Nohoch

A wide selection of colourful hammocks can be found at this address. Those who stay long enough in Mérida can have one made to order. *Calle 61 No. 499*

ACCOMMODATION

Caribe

A former monastery in the city centre, with a beautiful, green roof terrace. The restaurant serves Mexican food. *53 rooms, Calle 59 No. 500 (Parque Hidalgo), Tel. 0199/24 90 22, Fax 24 87 33, www.wotw.com/mexico/yuca-tan/hotels/hotelcaribe, category 2*

Dolores Alba

This small, family-run hotel is popular not only amongst those travelling on a budget. *50 rooms, Calle 63 No. 464, Tel. 0199/ 28 56 50, Fax 28 31 63, www. chichen-itza.com, category 2*

Hyatt Regency

Mérida's most exclusive address opened its doors in 1995. Stylish, large and centrally located. *300 rooms, Calle 60 No. 344/ Av. Colón, Tel. 0199/42 02 02, Fax 25 70 02, category 1*

Ballet Folklórico

Historical folk dances from pre-Columbian and colonial times. *Tues 9 pm, admission from approx. US $8, Teatro Peón Contreras*

Pancho's

The waiters wear costumes from the times of the Mexican Revolution; alternating entertainment shows. *Calle 59 No. 509/Calle 60–62*

Parque Santa Lucía

⚘ In this well-kept park, a concert is held every Thursday evening at 9 pm. *Calle 60/Calle 55*

INFORMATION

Aeroméxico

Plaza Americana, Calle 56 A No. 451, Tel. 0199/20 12 60

Tourist information

Peón Contreras Theatre, Calle 60/ Calle 57, Tel. 0199/24 93 89, Fax 28 65 48

SURROUNDING AREA

Chichén Itzá   (173/D2)

Only superlatives are able to describe this fantastic pre-Columbian city situated about 120 km east of Mérida. This is the most visited (and accessible) of all pre-Columbian sites on the whole continent. It was populated around AD 400 by the Maya and conquered by the Toltec-influenced Itzá around 1000. During the rule of their Toltec king Quetzalcóatl ('Plumed Serpent', the Toltec equivalent of the Mayan god 'Kukulcán'), the city was rebuilt in a synthesis of Toltec and Maya architecture.

The city is divided into two distinct parts, north and south, the

You should plan a whole day for Chichén Itzá

126

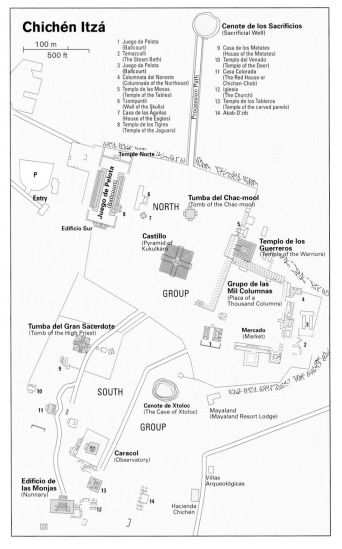

Chichén Itzá

100 m
500 ft

1 Juego de Pelota
  (Ballcourt)
2 Temazcalli
  (The Steam Bath)
3 Juego de Pelota
  (Ballcourt)
4 Columnata del Noreste
  (Columnade of the Northeast)
5 Templo de las Mesas
  (Temple of the Tables)
6 Tzompantli
  (Wall of the Skulls)
7 Casa de las Águilas
  (House of the Eagles)
8 Templo de los Tigres
  (Temple of the Jaguars)

Cenote de los Sacrificios
(Sacrificial Well)

9 Casa de los Metates
  (House of the Metates)
10 Templo del Venado
  (Temple of the Deer)
11 Casa Colorada
  (The Red House or
  Chichan-Chob)
12 Iglesia
  (The Church)
13 Templo de los Tableros
  (Temple of the carved panels)
14 Akab-D'zib

Procession Path

Temple Norte

P

Entry

Juego de Pelota
(Ballcourt)

6

8   7

NORTH

Edificio Sur

Tumba del Chac-mool
(Tomb of the Chac-mool)

5

Castillo
(Pyramid of
Kukulkán)

Templo de los
Guerreros
(Temple of the Warriors)

GROUP

Grupo de las
Mil Columnas
(Plaza of a
Thousand Columns)

4

Tumba del Gran Sacerdote
(Tomb of the High Priest)

9

10

11

SOUTH

GROUP

Mercado
(Market)

1

3

2

Cenote de Xtoloc
(The Cave of Xtoloc)

Mayaland
(Mayaland Resort Lodge)

Caracol
(Observatory)

13

12   14

Villas
Arqueológicas

Edificio de
las Monjas
(Nunnary)

Hacienda
Chichén

imposing and very famous Pyramid of Kukulcán *(El Castillo)* dominates the northern part of Chichén Itzá. The strange thing is that, in true pre-Columbian fashion, this pyramid was built on top of an older one. Tourists can enter a passage on the northern side of the structure that leads to the interior, where a jaguar throne and a Chac-Mool figure standing on top of the older, now covered

127

Pyramid climbing

When climbing pyramids, it's wise to exercise caution. Climbing to the top is usually easier than climbing down one. After enjoying the view, you will look down and see a vertiginous flight of steps, some uneven and damaged. It's best to avoid climbing pyramids under the blazing sun, but if you do, always wear a hat. If you suffer from vertigo, try to come down backwards so you don't have to look down, and brace yourself on the steps with both hands. The most visited pyramids have chains for people to hold on to.

pyramid await them. The 365 steps of the 30-m-high pyramid with nine terraces represent the days of the year. This is no coincidence, as the Maya were outstanding mathematicians and astronomers. At the foot of the steps are serpent heads, depicted with wide-open jaws. Twice every year (on 21 March and 23 September), the sun's rays shine on the pyramid in such a way that it looks as though a giant serpent is slowly slithering down the steps. This incredible spectacle draws thousands, so if you plan to attend, book your accommodation many months in advance.

In the vicinity of the Castillo is the large ball court *(juego de pelota)*, covering an area of 91 × 36 m, which makes it not only the nation's largest but also the best preserved. This popular game was taken very seriously by all pre-Columbian civilizations; the losers were often decapitated. The purpose of the game was to throw a rubber ball through the stone rings without using one's hands; two of the rings can still be seen along two of the 75-m-long delimiting walls; under the rings, a long line of wonderfully carved reliefs decorate the wall, and depict scenes of the game and the fate awaiting the losers. Two rows of seven persons

each, all expensively dressed and adorned, can clearly be seen — a masterpiece of stone carving.

Crossing the large square, one reaches the ◁▷ Temple of the Warriors *(Templo de los Guerreros)*, a building completely rebuilt by the Itzá to celebrate their victory. On top of a small, 12-m-high pyramid are delicately carved columns that originally supported a roof. The portal of the former Mayan temple, whose corbelled vault has since disappeared, consists of two massive columns recalling serpents. The rooms that the columns separated can still be discerned. At the entrance, an enigmatic Chac-Mool figure can be seen. These figures hold a bowl resting on their bellies, presumably for the palpitating hearts of the sacrificial victims. From here, there is a wonderful view of the Hall of the Thousand Columns below.

Several hundreds of metres to the north is the *Cenote Sagrado* (holy well), a steep, deep well with a diameter of 59 m. When Edward Thompson, the former American consul in Mérida started to excavate the site in the 1880s, he was so puzzled by the function of the cenote that he purchased it so he could dredge it! Soon enough, he found skeletons and many ceremonial and valuable objects at its depths, suggesting that human sacrifices were made. For the interested reader who would like to find out more about this fascinating and mysterious culture, the exciting and lavishly illustrated Penguin paperback *Maya: The Riddle and Rediscovery of a Lost Civilization* by Charles Gallenkamp is highly recommendable.

The most interesting structure of the southern group is the observatory, shaped like a snail-shell *(El Caracol)*. A small, spiral staircase leads to the top. It is believed that from here, Mayan priest-astronomers plotted the exact course of the Sun and Venus in order to predict good or bad harvests. *Daily 8 am–5 pm; in the winter, a light and sound show is held at 9 pm*

A good place to stay is the *Hotel Dolores Alba*, which has very comfortable rooms, air-conditioning and a swimming pool, 3 km before the entrance to the archaeological site (free transport). The buses from Mérida and Cancún stop in front of the hotel. *45 rooms, MEX 180, km 122, Tel. 0199/28 56 50, Fax 28 31 63, category 2*

Izamal (172/C2)

The small but charming colonial city of Izamal (pop. 35,000) has retained its charm precisely because it's not visited by masses of tourists. Surrounded by sisal fields, it lies 70 km east of Mérida and is referred to as the 'city of hills' and the 'city of three cultures'. The peculiarity of this place is that virtually all the town's buildings (churches, monasteries, even the gas station!) are painted yellow and white. The other unique characteristic is that most of the inhabitants use one-horse

carriages called *victorias* as their mode of transport.

Izamal is full of prehispanic relics, sometimes they can be seen forming parts of buildings or hidden under the vegetation. Like all major Mayan towns, it was reached by a *sacbeob*, a ceremonial road, linking it to other Mayan sites; a few remains of the ancient road can still be seen. Four blocks north of the *zócalo* lies the *Kinich-Kakmó Pyramid*, one of the continent's largest, built in honour of the sun god. The other important pyramid is *Kabul*, which was drawn in 1840 by famous architect-illustrator Frederick Catherwood, who, together with John Lloyd Stephens, re-discovered many of the Mayan ruins in the region. The other impressive structure is colonial: the town's giant monastery has an atrium covering an area of 8,000 square metres, the largest in Mexico. *San Antonio de Padua* was founded soon after the conquest, and in 1549 the Franciscan friar Diego de Landa moved in. A truly enigmatic and paradoxical figure, he was the most thorough destroyer of Mayan books that ever lived, but at the same time he wrote the first serious book about the great civilization that wrote those same books! More recently, Pope John Paul II met Indians from all the Americas in the giant atrium in 1993 (a photographic exhibition in the *monastic museum*). A tourist information office is located beside the monastery *(Glorieta Fray Diego de Landa)*.

Close to the *zócalo* are several modest restaurants. The *Kinich-Kakmó (category 3)* is only 50 m from the pyramid. Brightly coloured Indian handicrafts can be purchased in *Hecho a Mano (Calle 31 No. 323/*

Calle 34–36). Overnight stay at the guest house Canto, 15 rooms, Calle 30 No. 303 (town centre), category 3

Kabah   (172/C2–3)

This archaeological site hasn't been restored to the same extent as the others, but is nevertheless worth a visit in order to admire the Palace of the Masks *(Palacio de los Mascarones)*. The name says it all: the whole façade of the 46-m-long building is completely covered with reliefs depicting the face of the rain god Chac, an amazing 250 of them! Each mask is made up of 30 individual stones, an awesome achievement. Sadly, over the years, vandals have hacked away quite a few of the god's hooked noses.

Below the platform on which the palace stands, there is a cistern that served the purpose of providing water to the city's inhabitants, as there was no well. To the east lies the so-called *Judicial Palace* with countless decorative bundled columns. In front of the street lies the Central Group, most of it still largely unexcavated. Nevertheless, the free-standing and quite impressive *Arch* located in the outskirts of Kabah is the exception. The formerly decorated arch was built by the Maya to symbolize the beginning of a raised causeway that linked the city with neighbouring Uxmal, 15 km away. The highway was used for religious processions as well as for trade.

Labná   (172/C3)

Labná, only a short distance away from Kabah, is an important destination because of its famous *Mayan archway* with its beautifully restored corbelled vault. From a structure called *El Palacio*, a 170-m-long raised ceremonial road originates called *sacbé*, whose pavement is poorly restored. The road leads to the 5-m-high monumental arch once sketched by Catherwood – a very talented English draftsman who accompanied Stephens on his trips to countless Mayan ruins; his wonderful drawings illustrate his companion's classic *Incidents of Travel in Yucatán* in 1843. The *Arco*, built in the 8th/9th century in the Puuc style, is ornately decorated. Outstanding is the 'false vault' with its highly original construction. The arch is flanked by two rooms; above their entrances there is a beautiful frieze depicting knotted reeds and stylized Mayan huts. In some places, the original ochre colour of the arch can be discerned. On the return trip, you should by all means have a look at the *Palacio*, which is a fine example of an accomplished Puuc style, with its typical false columns, meander patterns and Chac masks.

Sayil   (172/C3)

Ten kilometres away from Kabah lies the archaeological site of Sayil, which draws the visitors with its 85 × 40 m large palace dating back to the 8th century *(El Palacio)*. This is truly a captivating structure, despite the fact that only the western side of it is fully restored. The upper two storeys are somewhat recessed, the middle one on its western side boasting four wide entrances supported by two bulbous columns. Behind them are two parallel rooms with a vaulted roof. The stone frieze above the entrances depicts the mask of the rain god, the figure

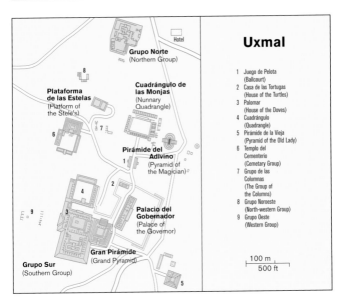

Uxmal

1 Juego de Pelota
  (Ballcourt)
2 Casa de las Tortugas
  (House of the Turtles)
3 Palomar
  (House of the Doves)
4 Cuadrángulo
  (Quadrangle)
5 Pirámide de la Vieja
  (Pyramid of the Old Lady)
6 Templo del
  Cementerio
  (Cemetary Group)
7 Grupo de las
  Columnas
  (The Group of
  the Columns)
8 Grupo Noroeste
  (North-western Group)
9 Grupo Oeste
  (Western Group)

100 m
500 ft

of a falling god as well as some stylized Mayan huts. Only the palace has been restored.

Uxmal (172/C2)

★ The temples of Uxmal (80 km south of Mérida), 'the ones built three times', belong to the masterpieces of the late Mayan classical period. The most important buildings of the 800 × 700 m site can be comfortably seen in a half-day. Immediately past the entrance, there is a *cistern* with three 'storeys', in which water that fell during the rain season was collected, since Uxmal lacked a natural well. The next structure, a very large one indeed, is the Pyramid of the Magician (*Pirámide del Adivino*), which according to legend was created in only one night by a magician. This 38-m-high structure has an oval plan formed by five substructures that were built

in stages during three centuries in such a way that a new structure was built on top of the old one every 52 years. At the foot of the pyramid, the remains of the first temple can be seen, two more are in the interior and can be reached via the steps and passages. The fourth temple is the best preserved of all, resembling a massive cube on which the fifth one stands.

By no means should you miss the imposing Palace of the Governor (*El Palacio del Gobernador*). The façade of the almost 100-m-long palace is decorated with an artistic stone frieze embellished with thousands of small mosaics, including 150 masks of the rain god Chac.

RIVIERA MAYA

(173/E2) From Cancún to the south, the road MEX 307 leads

131

to the holiday resorts on the Caribbean. The highway follows the coast and passes through fishing villages. Some of the coves *(caletas)* and beaches *(playas)* are only 2 to 7 km away and can be reached by secondary sandy or gravel roads. The 140-km stretch from Cancún to Tulum is called the Riviera Maya (formerly Turístico Tulum) and included, apart from small, varied archaeological sites, the fortified city of Tulum, built during the Mayan post-classical period.

The region is experiencing a boom in tourism owing to its promotion by the Ministry of Tourism and private investors. Picturesque holiday resorts on the beach, modest *cabañas* as well as luxurious bungalows, nature preserves, water-sports facilities and leisure parks have already been established. The film *Against All Odds* (title song by superstar Phil Collins) was filmed here and captures the most romantic spots.

SIGHTS

Akumal

This place situated about 25 km north of Tulum became well known thanks to the discovery of the Spanish galleon *Señora de los Milagros*, which sank just off the coast in 1714. Tourists enjoy the warm, turquoise waters of the picturesque cove as well as the outstanding underwater sights. Akumal is the base of the Cedam group, a club whose task is the discovery and securing of sunken ships as well as the pursuit of underwater archaeology (the club also runs a museum).

Playa del Carmen

This beach, located half-way between Tulum and Cancún, has been a favourite destination amongst individual and backpack tourists, although who knows how long it will remain that, as it is growing very fast, especially after the opening of two holiday resorts and an 18-hole golf course. Slowly but surely, the packaged tours of holidaymakers are coming here, enjoying the more relaxed atmosphere and gorgeous, powdery, white, sandy beaches. Restaurants, cafés and hotels are located along the beaches. Along the town's main street, ironically called 'Fifth Avenue' *(5a Avenida)*, you meet everybody either having breakfast or window-shopping in the various handcrafts shops and boutiques. The town teems with tourists only when a large cruise ship anchors off the coast and the passengers flood the place.

Puerto Aventuras

Hard to believe, but true: a holiday resort as large as the city it is situated in: the new, luxurious resort 30 km south of Playa del Carmen with its marina, golf courses, hotels and numerous holiday flats is the perfect place for the well-to-do. Beware of the pushy 'time sharing' sales agents who seem to populate the village. But if you manage to shake them off, you will enjoy one of the most beautiful and romantic Caribbean spots, the perfect combination of tropical beach and luxurious resort.

Tulum

Perched high atop a white limestone cliff 12 m above the azure

Tulum – a unique and magnificent location above the turquoise sea

Caribbean, the ruins of Tulum are unique not only because of their unparalleled location but also because they are the only fortified Mayan city. The site is architecturally unimportant, but it has the distinction of having been one of very few Mayan cities inhabited at the arrival of the Spaniards, who upon seeing this magnificent city 'as splendid as Seville' from their ships in 1518, prudently decided not to land. The city was built in the postclassical period around AD 1000 as a trade port, and the name means 'wall' or 'fortress', referring to the fact that it was surrounded by a massive protective wall, whose remains can still be seen. Another name that appears in old Spanish chronicles is Zama – meaning 'sunrise' – and, indeed, the ancient master builders chose an ideal spot, where the first rays of the sun reach the city in the east.

A small 'tourist railway' takes tourists from the visitor centre and the carpark to the site (about 1 km away). The western gate, the only one left of five, leads to the centre of the temple area surrounded by a high wall. Almost four dozen structures can be visited. The most beautiful of these is the one reproduced in countless postcards, ✧ *El Castillo*, reached via a wide flight of steps. The exertion is well worth it: from the top, there's an unforgettable view of the site, the cliffs, the ocean and the small cove below. Everywhere are beautiful butterflies, green geckoes and flying pelicans. Before leaving, don't miss the temple's entrance columns, which recall three coiled serpents. In the interior, some remains of once glorious frescoes can be seen.

Afterwards, you should walk over to the northern Temple of the Descending God *(Templo del*

Dios Descendente). The small niche above the entrance depicts a very special god: Ab Muzen Cab, the god of bees, with his head inclined towards the ground. Inside, a small opening is flanked by two stony benches. For scientists, however, the most important building is the Temple of the Frescoes *(Templo de los Frescos)* in the middle of the ancient city. All its walls were painted, depicting gods, flowers and animals, each scene framed by geometric lines decorated with serpents. An exterior roof frieze on the western side of the temple portrays the bee god once again, this time in triple execution.

Xcaret

An eco-archaeological park 5 km south of Playa del Carmen suitable for all children between the ages of 7 and 70. This tropical nature park was built around a lagoon on the site of a former Mayan ceremonial centre. Exactly on the same spot where long ago the Maya waited to be taken to the temples by boat, nowadays many open-air restaurants wait for their customers. The facility is reached by walking through a small *museum* showing the folklore and the fauna of the area. Quite exciting is swimming in one of the many underground rivers typical of Yucatán. The visitors wear their pink life jackets, paddling hundreds of metres into the cave and through the clear waters. There are also interesting things to explore above the ground, such as swimming in the turquoise *cove* or snorkelling in the clear waters whilst being surrounded by all kinds of colourful fish. An *aquarium* as well as several restored Mayan structures can also be visited. *Mayan temples, daily 10 am–6 pm, admission US $39, a bus tour can also be booked from Cancún*

RESTAURANTS

The place to stroll is 'Fifth Avenue' in Playa del Carmen with its highly fluctuating clientele. It's best to sit where many others already are. In addition, there are numerous open-air restaurants directly on the beach.

SHOPPING

Plaza Marina Playacar

Countless arts-and-crafts shops under one roof, plus a pharmacy and coffee shop; car and diving gear hire. *At the mole of Playa del Carmen*

ACCOMMODATION

South of Tulum, along the beach, there are numerous small, family-run hostels and *cabaña* facilities with modest, but romantic, furnishings. Recommended are the *Cabañas Chac Mool (km 5.3).*

Acuario

Tulum now has a good, three-star hotel so it is now possible to visit the ruins early in the morning before the crowds arrive. *37 rooms, Crucero Ruinas de Tulum, Tel. 01987/120 61, no Fax, category 2*

Jungla Caribe

Located at the 'Fifth Avenue', not far from the beach, this new hotel offers an enchanting, green inner courtyard with pool. The facility has been exquisitely furnished and the large rooms are tastefully decorated. The (Italian) restaurant is the town's best. With beach club 'El Faro'. Highly recommended. *26 rooms, 5a Av./Calle 8, Playa del Carmen, Tel./Fax 01987/306 50, category 2*

Las Palapas

In a private nature preserve 1 km north of Playa del Carmen and on the beach lies this romantic and comfortable facility with a fresh-water pool. *6 cabañas on the beach and 49 rooms surrounded by greenery. Playa del Carmen, km 292.5, Tel. 01987/ 306 16, Fax 304 58, category 1*

SPORTS

The largest selection of water sports by far can be found in *Puerto Aventuras.* There are also good possibilities in *Playa del Carmen.*

INFORMATION

Tourist information

Playa del Carmen, 5a Av./Av. Juárez (kiosk at the plaza)

SURROUNDING AREA

Cobá   (173/E2)

★ Forty kilometres north-west of Tulum, surrounded by a tropical jungle and scattered amongst five lakes, are the Mayan ruins of Cobá. During the rainy season, the pyramids and temples are hidden in the lush, tropical vegetation. But during the dry season, they stand out when the surrounding vegetation has dried out. The ceremonial centre was built in the classical style between AD 600 and 900. It is believed that up to 40,000 people once lived here, even after the arrival of the Spaniards. Incredibly, Cobá was never found by them.

The extended site has five building groups that can be visited. You first walk by the group bearing the same name as the site, located between two lakes. It is dominated by a 24-m-high pyramid called *La Iglesia* (the church). Almost twice as high is another pyramid belonging to the Nohoch Mul group (2 km to the north-east), which goes by

Either fully equipped or just with a snorkel and flippers: the Yucatecan coastline of the Riviera Maya is an ideal place for a diving adventure

You can safely explore Sian Ka'an by boat – and leave your fears at home: wildlife is not permitted to be taken aboard

the name of *El Castillo*, of which 128 steps lead to the ⚜ top. The strenuous climb is well worth it, as the panoramic view is spellbinding. The entrance to the temple on top is decorated with a figure of the bee god. Those who would like to explore the other, unrestored groups, partly covered by vegetation, of Las Pinturas, Macanxoc and Chumuc Mul can do so. In the Macanxoc group and between the large lake of the same name and the smaller one of Sacalpuc are the remains of a centuries-old paved road, a *sacbé*.

The best place to spend the night is in the hotel *Villa Arqueológica (40 rooms, at the lake, Tel./Fax 01987/420 87, category 2)*, a two-storeyed patio-hotel belonging to the Club Méditerranée; good atmosphere. In the evenings, you can hear the chirping of the crickets and the croaking of the frogs from the nearby lake. Other accommodation is considerably more modest.

Sian Ka'an (173/E3)

Covering half a million hectares, this biosphere reserve has been classified by the UNESCO as being particularly worthy of protection. It is one of the country's largest and most fascinating nature preserves. Sian Ka'an ('begin of the sky') is an important coastal ecosystem of great interest to scientists, as it has untouched tropical jungle, wetlands, lagoons and coral reefs, making it an ideal habitat for pumas, jaguars, monkeys, crocodiles and nesting sea turtles. More than 350 bird species have been catalogued, and the marine life is no less abundant. In addition, 30 minor Mayan ruins have already been discovered within.

One road crosses the reserve, and primitive accommodation awaits the adventurous visitor. Day trips with motor boats from Cancún are offered by an organization called *Amigos de Sian Ka'an (US $80 per person, Tel. 0198/84 95 83, Fax 87 30 88)*.

Wilderness and whales, jungles and waterfalls

These routes are marked in green on the map on the inside front cover and in the Road Atlas beginning on page 150

① COLONIAL CITIES IN THE CENTRAL HIGHLANDS

 Travel through Mexico City, Tlaxcala, Puebla, Cuernavaca, Taxco and Toluca. In Puebla, you will get a good glimpse of a magnificent colonial city, whilst neighbouring Tlaxcala shows a more Indian face and serves as a good contrast. Silent witnesses of early colonial times are the former sugarcane plantation of Cocoyoc, once the property of Cortés and now a luxurious hotel, and the palace of the conquistador in Cuernavaca. More colonial highpoints are the Spanish cities of Taxco and Toluca. Recommended accommodation can be found in Puebla, Cocoyoc or Cuernavaca, so that the tour (a total of almost 600 km) can be accomplished in five, well-planned days.

Drive out of Mexico City towards the east and soon you will reach the MEX 190D highway (a toll road, 'cuota' in Spanish) which offers magnificent views of the majestic twin volcanoes of Popocatépetl and Ixtaccíhuatl. After 130 km, you will reach Puebla. Shortly before getting there, at km 100 in San Martín Texmelucan, be sure to take the 25-km-long road to the north, which will take you to the charming city of *Tlaxcala.* The road branches off from the highway and climbs to the 2,400-m-high provincial state capital (pop. 60,000) of the tiny state with the same name. Soon after reaching the Mexican highlands, the conquistadors started erecting a city, right in the middle of the territory of their allies, the Tlaxcaltecs, passionate enemies of the Aztecs, whose help greatly contributed to the collapse of the Aztec Empire. The buildings bordering the *zócalo* are exquisitely restored, especially the *Palacio del Gobierno* (1530) with its ornate façade and attractive windows and doors; the interior contains large *murales* depicting the history of the Tlaxcaltecs. Opposite it stands the *Palacio de Justicia*, recognized by its clocktower. The Baroque exterior of the *Parroquia* (parish church) is decorated with Puebla tiles. Crossing the Plaza Xicoténcatl towards the south, you reach the *Convento de San Francisco* (1540), a former Franciscan monastery with a good view of the city, which now houses the *local history museum.* In the adjoining Church of San Francisco,

Cortés baptized the first Indian chiefs. Two kilometres east of the city, on top of a hill, stands the *Santuario de Ocotlán,* an 18th-century Baroque church famous for its exceptional beauty.

On road 119, after only 24 km, you will reach *Puebla (page 53).* You should spend a whole day seeing all the interesting sights, the numerous attractive hotels and restaurants.

On the road from Puebla to the south (MEX 190), follow the road that branches off (20 km) and leads to *Cholula* and its impressive pyramid *(page 55)*; visit the nearby church of *Tonantzintla (page 55)* and the small village church (built in the Poblano style with colourful tiles) of *San Francisco de Acatepec,* only a few kilometres away.

The health resort of *Cuautla* (pop. 175,000; altitude 1,300 m) is popular amongst the locals. It has been a health resort since colonial times; the sulphurous waters of Agua Hedionda are especially recommended. Further on, on the outskirts of Cuautla, lies the luxurious hotel *Hacienda Cocoyoc (315 rooms, km 32, Carretera Cuautla–Cuernavaca, Tel. 01735/612 11, Fax 612 12, category 1),* a preferred holiday destination amongst Mexican VIPs and foreign tourists. It is said that Cortés had it built. The extensive, beautiful tropical grounds have a small aqueduct and a waterfall, making the hotel one of the nation's most stylish places to stay.

In *Cuernavaca (page 46)*, the colonial homes with peaceful patios and the mild, spring-like climate (altitude: 1,540 m) lure visitors to take a stroll and explore this hilly city. On the outskirts is the *Pyramid of Teopanzolco.*

From Cuernavaca, the toll road MEX 95D will take you to the more southern city of *Taxco (page 61)*: the narrow cobbled streets of this charming silver city are lined with silver and crafts shops. Aldous Huxley and German naturalist Alexander von Humboldt were delighted by the unforgettable views, especially at dusk.

Before returning to Mexico City, there's one more opportunity of admiring colonial architecture: *Toluca,* the capital (pop. 500,000) of the state of México, at an altitude of almost 2,700 m, once more shows the architectural virtuosity of the former colonial masters. The Aztec city of Tollocán has buildings that date back mostly to the 18th and 19th centuries, which have been well restored by the city fathers of this prosperous city. Many of them house museums; of particular interest is the *Museo Numismático (Tues–Sat 10 am–6 pm, Av. Hidalgo Poniente 506),* which occupies a magnificent 19th-century mansion, where a famous collection of Latin American coins is on display. The *Museo José María Velasco (Tues–Sun 10 am–6 pm, Av. Lerdo de Tejada Poniente 400)* is also worth a visit. Many drawings and some canvases of the famous landscape painter are exhibited here. In the city centre, newer buildings were given a layer of red sandstone so they would blend with their surroundings. The walkways under the arcades protect from the rain or sun — those of the *Plaza Fray Andrés de Castro* are particularly beautiful.

From Toluca, take the toll road MEX 15D back to Mexico City, 60 km away.

② THE TRANSPENINSULA IN BAJA CALIFORNIA

Deserts, mountains and beaches – from Tijuana to Cabo San Lucas. The 1,300-km-long peninsula has been opened up by the paved road called Carretera Transpeninsular (MEX 1); it is an astounding 1,600 kilometres from the northern border at Tijuana to the extreme southern tip of Cabo San Lucas. Certain stretches of it follow the eastern and western coastlines, others remain in the interior. Most visitors drive a rented car or their own caravan, but first-class buses also serve the route. Although Baja California has some interesting prehistoric rock paintings, romantic colonial villages and isolated Jesuit missions, the main attraction is the stark beauty of the arid mountain landscape as well as the pristine, isolated beaches of the long peninsula with their varied fauna. Until recently, this part of Mexico was accessible only by sea or air. You should plan at least one week for the interesting but arduous journey.

The hectic border metropolis of *Tijuana* (pop. 1 million) *(page 90)* quickly vanishes as you drive south on the modern highway; after 110 km, you will reach the harbour of *Ensenada* (pop. 200,000) situated at the end of the large, semicircular Bahía Todos los Santos. Fishing and tourism are the city's two main industries. *Whale watching tours* are offered between November and March. In the other months of the year, you should visit the interesting *Museo de Ciencia,* specializing in grey whales.

Sixteen kilometres south of Ensenada (19 km), take the road that branches off, crossing the peninsula of *Punta la Banda* (which closes the southern half of the bay) to *La Bufadora.* Here, seawater funnels into an underwater cave and is forced up through a small hole, a kind of marine 'Old Faithful'.

The road to the south reaches El Rosario on the western coast, then it turns into the interior, crossing a desert full of many different types of cactus, amongst them the impressive, huge saguaro *(órgano).* After crossing 570 km of this desert characterized by the spiny drought-resistant vegetation, you will reach the town of *Guerrero Negro,* the site of the well-known *Parque Natural de la Ballena Gris,* in whose coastal lagoons marine biologists and tourists can observe whales as they mate.

MEX 1 traverses the peninsula once again and, after 150 km, it reaches the *oasis San Ignacio.* A former Jesuit mission offers overnight accommodation; the palm groves invite drivers and passengers alike to stretch their legs. After another 70 km, the town of *Santa Rosalía* (pop. 15,000) on the eastern coast will appear on the horizon (ferry service to Guaymas across the Gulf). The town was founded by French miners who lived from copper extraction. At the centre, look out for a church of pre-fabricated iron designed by A. Eiffel. Nowadays, it's the meeting place of deep-sea fishermen.

Two hundred kilometres to the south lies the resort town of *Loreto (page 89)* on the east coast. Afterwards, the road takes turns into the interior, then towards the west coast – a side trip to *San Carlos (page 90)* is recommended – finally reaching *La Paz (page 89)* after 350 km. From here, drive another 180 km until you reach *San José del Cabo.* A further 33 km will take you to the peninsula's southern tip of *Cabo San Lucas (page 86).*

Natural spectacles and pre-Columbian sites: from the Cañón del Sumidero to the Gulf of Mexico. Leaving Tuxtla Gutiérrez towards the east, after 30 km you will reach the small city of Chiapa de Corzo, starting point for the boat tours to the Cañón del Sumidero. Afterwards, the Pan-American Highway zigzags its way up the steep mountains until, after 50 km, it reaches the colonial city and unofficial Indian capital of San Cristóbal de Las Casas. From there, MEX 199 crosses the northern mountains on its way to tropical Palenque (220 km). After another 140 km to the north-west you will reach Villahermosa. You should spend the night in San Cristóbal and Palenque; since you can take the plane to Mérida from Villahermosa, you should plan at least four days for this trip.

Tuxtla Gutiérrez, the modern capital of Chiapas, is soon left behind. After a stroll around the plaza of *Chiapa de Corzo (page 106)*, walk to the river bank and take the boat for a very interesting trip to the *Cañón del Sumidero (page 106)*, which will take several hours. Afterwards, it is still possible to reach scenic *San Cristóbal de Las Casas (page 104)* high in the mountains, where numerous colonial houses offer attractive overnight accommodation. This magnificent city, with its glorious Indian heritage and its profusion of arts and crafts, tempts you to stay more than one day.

During the journey from San Cristóbal (2,140 m) to Palenque (200 m), you will pass Ocosingo, where a road (14 km) branches off to *Toniná*. This former *Mayan ceremonial centre* has only recently been excavated. The site has a small *museum*. The main pyramid with the large temple on top resembles a hill. Most of the structures are still covered by lush vegetation. The unusual feature of Toniná ('stony house') are its large, round boulders, many of which were beautifully carved by the Maya. Sixty kilometres away from Palenque, and only 4 km away from the main road, lie the splendid multiple waterfalls of *Agua Azul (page 102)*, an ideal spot for picnicking. Twenty kilometres before reaching Palenque, the 30-m-high waterfall of *Misol-há* forms an inviting pool surrounded by lush, tropical vegetation (swimming permitted).

You must spend the night in *Palenque (page 99)* so that you can admire this impressive *archaeological site*. If you wish to visit *Bonampak (page 102)* and *Yaxchilán (page 103)*, you should add one or two days to your trip.

The drive from Palenque to Villahermosa, the capital of Tabasco, crosses a tropical landscape criss-crossed by swamps, lagoons and rivers; the climate is hot and humid. The small state of Tabasco has become prosperous owing to the oil deposits found there; in recent years, cattle and agriculture (cocoa, bananas, sugarcane, coconuts) have joined that industry. If you manage to leave Palenque very early in the morning, you'll be able to reach *Villahermosa (page 112)* early enough to visit *Parque La Venta,* with its Olmec sculptures and heads, in the morning, and the *CICOM museum* in the afternoon. In the early evening, you can still reach Tuxtla Gutiérrez (bus, plane) and Mérida (plane).

Practical information

Useful addresses and indispensable tips
for your visit to Mexico

ADMISSION PRICES

You should plan to pay between US $2 and 4 for admission into important museums and archaeological sites. Bear in mind that there may be an extra charge to take in camera and video equipment with you. Admission is sometimes free on Sundays, and, at small sites and museums, is generally US $1.50.

AMERICAN & BRITISH ENGLISH

Marco Polo travel guides are written in British English. In North America, certain terms and usages deviate from British usage. Some of the more frequently encountered examples are:
baggage for luggage, billion for milliard, cab for taxi, car rental for car hire, drugstore for chemist's, fall for autumn, first floor for groundfloor, freeway/highway for motorway, gas(oline) for petrol, railroad for railway, restroom for toilet/lavatory, streetcar for tram, subway for underground/tube, toll-free numbers for freephone numbers, trailer for caravan, trunk for boot, vacation for holiday, wait staff for waiting staff (in restaurants etc.), zip code for postal code.

BANKS

Money exchange
The symbol for the peso ($) is the same as that for the dollar, so make sure you know what currency is meant when looking at prices. You can exchange your money in *bureaux de change* (only in the big cities) or in hotels. The Mexico City airport offers the best exchange rate.

Credit cards and cheques
Travellers' cheques in US dollars are recommended, and small US dollar notes are often very useful. Larger hotels and car rental companies accept all major credit cards, the same can be said of expensive shops and restaurants in the cities.

BUSES

The *autobús*, in Mexico often called *camión*, reaches virtually every city and town several times a day. Many private bus companies operate in the country, and they offer their efficient services in three classes: third-class *(local)* buses are ancient vehicles that go to every little town and stop for every passenger. Second-class *(segunda)* buses connect larger cities, but they are old, slow and stop often; there is no advance booking so they are always crowded. Try to board at the city of departure. The first-class buses *(lujo, primera, espreso, rápido)* connect the larger cities non-stop; reservations are a must; buses are air-conditioned; no standing passengers; purchase the ticket the day before. Bus stations *(camionera, estación de autobuses, central de autobuses)* are often on the outskirts of towns and are usually divided into classes and bus companies.

CAMPING

Camp sites are geared to the American and Canadian tourist and their motor caravans. Genuine camp sites are rare. The Mexican Tourist Office provides a list. For personal safety reasons, by all means avoid camping on the beach or in the forest!

CAR RENTAL

In addition to the multinational car-rental companies, several local companies offer lower prices, but check the car thoroughly before signing. Your driving license is valid, but an international one is advantageous if you get into trouble. Use your credit card to avoid the high deposit fees. Obey every single traffic law and sign (even if the locals don't), as Mexican policemen use every possible excuse to stop you for a motoring offence. Remember, they are badly paid and take advantage of receiving money (the famous 'mordida' mentioned before) in return for dismissing the offence. It is better to pay them something than be forced to drive to police headquarters, where you will certainly have to pay a lot more.

CUSTOMS

The following articles may be brought into the country duty-free: 400 cigarettes or 250 g of pipe tobacco; 3 litres of wine or spirits; a reasonable amount of perfume or eau de toilette; 2 photo, movie or video cameras for non-residents as well as 12 unexposed rolls of film or video cassettes for each camera and goods amounting to up to US $300 or an equivalent amount in another currency.

DOMESTIC FLIGHTS

Mexico boasts almost 50 airports of all sizes; the major airlines, Mexicana and Aeroméxico, and smaller ones offer scheduled flights to most of them. With Mexicana's and Aeroméxico's Mexi-Pass, it is possible to fly to certain cities with large discounts.

EMBASSIES

British Embassy
Río Lerma 71,
Colonia Cuauhtémoc,
06500 México, DF, Mexico,
Tel. 5/207 20 89,
Fax 5/207 76 72
www.embajadabritanica.com. mx
E-mail:
infogen@embajadabritanica. com.mx

Canadian Embassy
Apartado Postal 105-05,
11560 México, DF, Mexico,
Tel. 5/724 79 00,
Fax 5/724 79 80 (administration)
www.canada.org.mx

American Embassy
Paseo de la Reforma 305,
06500 México, DF, Mexico,
Tel. 5/211 00 42,

Fax 5/511 99 80,
www.usembassy.org.mx

FERRIES

A ferry service operates between the Baja Peninsula and the Mexican mainland from La Paz to Mazatlán (16 hours), from Cabo San Lucas to Puerto Vallarta (18 hours), from Santa Rosalía to Guaymas (7 hours) and from La Paz to Topolobampo/Los Mochis (8 hours). Since privatization, service to some ports has been discontinued. Book in advance if you intend to take your car. In the Caribbean, a ferry service operates between Cozumel and Isla Mujeres to the mainland.

HEALTH

There are no vaccination requirements. However, it is advisable to obtain protection against malaria for jungle regions lower than 600 m. Typhoid fever and hepatitis are common, so take precautions. For the tropical areas, don't forget your sun cream and insect repellent. Steer clear of tap water, ice cream, non-bottled beverages, raw vegetables and unpeeled fruit. If you come down with 'Montezuma's Revenge', the Mexican medication Lomotil is very effective and widely available.

The Mexican pharmacy is called *farmacia* and, apart from medicines, also sells household goods and cigarettes(!). All major medicines are widely sold and often cheaper than they are in other countries; they're just as good and available mostly without prescription. In case of a medical or dental emergency, turn to the hotel receptionist.

In Mexico City, the US-American hospital has its own ambulance for emergencies: *ABC-Hospital, Col. America, Tel. 01 52 77 50 00.* In the capital: *Tel. 515 83 59* and *516 80 70,* in other parts of the country, call the local *Cruz Roja* or *Centro de Salud.*

INFORMATION

Secretaría de Turismo
Also acts as arbitration board in case of disagreements with hotels, car rental companies, etc. *Av. Presidente Masaryk 172, Col. Polanco, 11580 México D.F., Tel. 015/250 85 55 or 250 01 23,*

Free emergency phone and information service in English and Spanish, around the clock. *Tel. 01/800/903 92.*

Fondo Nacional de Fomento al Turismo (FONATUR)
17th Floor, Insurgentes Sur 800, Colonia del Valle, 03100 México, DF, Mexico,

---

Earthquakes

Owing to its geographical location (all of Mexico's west coast and the central highlands are in the 'Ring of Fire'), Mexico City is unavoidably earthquake-prone. Indeed, every year hundreds of imperceptible mini-earthquakes occur, and dangerous earthquakes, such as the one that hit Mexico City in 1985 or Puebla in 1999, are fortunately rare. Mexican architects and civil engineers are amongst the most experienced in designing earthquake-proof structures.

Tel. 5/687 26 97
or 250/01 23 01 53 (travel hotline),
Fax 5/682 50 58

in Canada:
Mexican Government Tourism office
*Suite 1801, 2 Bloor Street West,
Toronto, Ontario M4W 3E2,
Tel. 416/925 0704
or 1-800/44 63 94 26 toll-free in
Canada and the USA,
Fax 416/925 60 61,
E-mail: mexgo3@inforam.net*

in the UK:
Mexican Ministry of Tourism
*2nd Floor, 60-61 Trafalgar Square,
London WC2N 5DS,
Tel. 0171/734 10 58,
Fax 0171/930 92 02, E-mail:
mexicanministry@easynet.co.uk*

in the United States:
**Mexican Government
Tourism Office**
*Suite 1401, 405 Park Avenue,
New York, NY 10022,
Tel. 212/755 72 61
or 1-800/446 39 42 toll-free in
the USA and Canada,
Fax 212/755 28 74*

LANGUAGE

The official language is Spanish,
but some slang words are of Indian
origin. English is widely spoken in
areas well frequented by tourists.

MEASURES & WEIGHTS

1 cm	0.39 inches
1 m	1.09 yards (3.28 feet)
1 km	0.62 miles
1 m^2	1.20 sq. yards
1 ha	2.47 acres
1 km^2	0.39 sq. miles
1 g	0.035 ounces
1 kg	2.21 pounds

1 British tonne	1016 kg
1 US ton	907 kg
1 litre is equivalent to 0.22 Imperial gallons and 0.26 US gallons	

OPENING HOURS

Businesses in provincial Mexico
have the obligatory early afternoon
break (usually from 1 to 4 pm), but
to compensate for this, they remain
open until 8 or 9 pm. There are no
fixed hours of business. Banks are
usually open *Mon–Fri 9 am–1 pm,*
the post office *Mon–Fri 9 am–6 pm.*
Museums close on Mondays.

PASSPORT & VISA

British citizens need a passport valid for at least six months to enter
Mexico. For Canadians and Americans some proof of identity with
photo is sufficient. The majority
of European tourists land at the
Benito Juárez International Airport in Mexico City. First of all,
you must show the filled-out
tourist card to the Mexican immi-
gration authorities, which can be
obtained from a Mexican embassy,
consulate or the airline. The
stamped copy remains in the passport, and it is very important not to
lose it, as it must be shown again
when leaving the country. Minors
under 18 years of age, travelling
with only one parent, need written
and notarized permission from the
other parent to enter the country.
Once you are spotted as a tourist,
many unauthorized taxi drivers
will approach you. Although their
fares are lower, for personal secur-
ity reasons, you should go to a
ticket window for the authorized
airport taxis, where the prices are
fixed and you pay according to district. The taxis are yellow and bear

an airplane symbol. The fare to the hotel should be US $10 to 12.

Some 300 m from exit A is the entrance to the underground, but luggage is not allowed on the trains.

PHOTOGRAPHY

Take as much film as you can with you (it is more expensive in Mexico). Be prepared to pay an extra fee to take photos in some archaeological sites. As a rule, Indians don't enjoy being photographed, so it is necessary to ask them for permission, which they may give provided you pay them for posing. In some regions (especially Chiapas), it pays to be extra careful.

POLICE

Ironically, uniformed policemen have been known to be involved in criminal acts. According to the latest news reports, policemen have been increasingly involved in robberies and other criminal activities. Therefore, try to avoid contact with local policemen. In case of trouble, better turn to the blue-uniformed tourist police or the highway police ('Policía de Caminos y Puentes'); they are usually accessible and friendly.

POST (CORREO) & TELEPHONE

The post office is called *correo*; a postcard sent via air mail *(por avión)* costs about 3 pesos.

Public telephones are numerous. You can use telephone cards of 30, 50 and 100 pesos. Luckily, it's not necessary to use the very expensive hotel phones or those of the telephone company office.

International calls:
to USA and Canada: 001,
to the UK 0044, to Mexico 0052.

RAILWAY

The Mexican railway system (more than 25,000 km) extends from the US border to Mérida in Yucatán; most of it is still run by the inefficient, state-owned company Ferrocarriles Nacionales de México. It is by far the cheapest mode of transportation in the country, but not very comfortable, as it is slow and often not on time. There are some better routes and first class service, though: from Mexico City to Guadalajara, San Miguel de Allende, Morelia and Veracruz.

TAXIS

When the taximeter is running, the fare is comparatively low. If not, be sure that you agree on the price. Check at the hotel for current fares. In Mexico City, board only a safe radio taxi ('taxi de sitio').

TIME

GMT minus 6 hours, in the western states minus 7 or 8 hours. Summer time begins on the first Sunday in April and ends the last Sunday in October.

TIPPING

In a restaurant, 10 to 15 % is common. Taxi drivers don't expect a tip. But for small favours, 2 or 3 pesos are generally appreciated.

VOLTAGE

110/125V, American flat plug.

WATER TEMPERATURES

On the west coast 24 to 28°C (75 to 82°F), on the Gulf of Mexico

(Veracruz) 24 to 26°C (75 to 79°F), and on the Caribbean (Cancún) 25° to 28°C (77 to 82°F).

WHEN TO GO

The rainy season takes place from late May to late October, and the dry season predominates the rest of the year. In the central highlands, the rain often falls in heavy downpours only in the afternoons, but in Chiapas and along the Caribbean, greater amounts fall. Temperatures depend on the altitude, from hot and humid on the coast to cold nights above 2,000 m. For this reason, the mild or non-existent Mexican winter is recommended, but avoid Christmas and Easter.

YOUTH HOSTELS

A total of 70 youth hostels belonging to various organizations are scattered throughout Mexico, but usually in cities or resorts. The Mexican Tourist Office provides a current list. The best ones are in the southern part of Mexico City (with a view of the Popocatépetl) and in Cancún (directly on the beach).

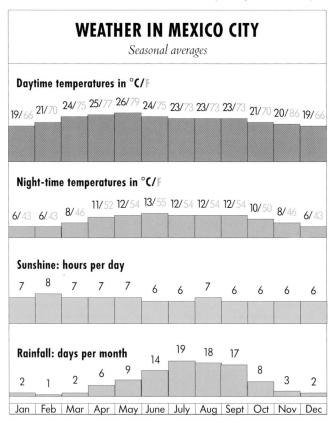

WEATHER IN MEXICO CITY

Seasonal averages

Daytime temperatures in °C/F

19/66 21/70 24/75 25/77 26/79 24/75 23/73 23/73 23/73 21/70 20/86 19/66

Night-time temperatures in °C/F

6/43 6/43 8/46 11/52 12/54 13/55 12/54 12/54 12/54 10/50 8/46 6/43

Sunshine: hours per day

7 8 7 7 7 6 6 7 6 6 6 6

Rainfall: days per month

2 1 2 6 9 14 19 18 17 8 3 2

| Jan | Feb | Mar | Apr | May | June | July | Aug | Sept | Oct | Nov | Dec |

Do's and don'ts!

*How to avoid some of the pitfalls
that face the unwary traveller*

Visiting a 'factory'

Sooner or later, all participants of a tour, whether it lasts a week or just a day, will be taken to a time-consuming visit of a *factory* so they can purportedly see how the beautiful arts and crafts are made by the Indians. Whilst this may in some cases be true, the owner of the factory is invariably a 'friend' of the courier or tourist guide and the pretty crafts are therefore sold at a discount (the reality is often just the opposite). So, avoid this trap with a polite but firm 'No, gracias!'

Second-class buses on long journeys

Although second-class buses may look like a tempting alternative to their first-class counterparts, they are no bargain after all: they're almost always bursting full, stop everywhere and therefore the journey takes forever. So, always travel *primera clase* and purchase your ticket in advance (still a bargain!); your seat is guaranteed, there are no people standing inside, the bus (which is cleaner) does not stop between cities and the journey is (usually) safer.

How is your Spanish?

Since Mexico and the USA are so different from one another and, throughout history, their relationship has been marked by both cooperation and all-out war (don't forget that in the mid-19th century, the USA took Texas and the Southwestern states by force), it is only natural that Mexicans have an ambivalent attitude to the *gringos*, as Americans are called. The Mexican admires American technology and the American way of life, but he is also envious and resentful and certainly does not enjoy being treated like a second-class citizen. And if things are not always as efficient as at home, take it in stride – no country is perfect. Mexicans will greatly appreciate the effort of foreigners to communicate their wishes in Spanish and to show admiration for the country's glorious past and present achievements.

Drugs

Mexico illegally exports great quantities of drugs to the USA, much to the northern neighbour's distress. But this doesn't mean that drugs are legal or tolerated. Quite the contrary: the drug laws are harsh and the penalties severe. Don't be tempted and don't ruin your holiday; the very last place you'd like to end up is in a Mexican jail! If you have to bring a lot of medication into the country, be prepared to prove that it has been prescribed by a doctor.

147

ROAD ATLAS LEGEND

Autobahn	Motorway
Autobahn in Bau	Motorway under construction
Autobahn in Planung	Motorway projected
Durchgangsstraße	Thoroughfare
Durchgangsstraße in Bau	Thoroughfare under construction
Wichtige Hauptstraße	Important main road
Wichtige Hauptstraße in Bau	Important main road under construction
Hauptstraße	Main road
Hauptstraße in Bau	Main road under construction
Sonstige Straße	Other road
⑤ ⑩ ⑧ Straßennummern	Road numbers
218 Großkilometer	Long distances in km
54 Kleinkilometer	Short distances in km
26 Kleinkilometer an der Autobahn	Short distances in km along the motorway
Carretera Panamericana Touristenstraße	Tourist route
Straße gegen Gebühr befahrbar	Toll road
Eisenbahn	Railway
● Autofähre	Car ferry
Schiffahrtslinie	Shipping route
Periodischer Fluß	Seasonal river
Staatsgrenze	National boundary
Verwaltungrenze	Administrative boundary

Kultur
Culture

★★ <u>Oaxaca</u>
★★ *Chichén Itza*   Eine Reise wert / Worth a journey

★ **Mérida**
★ *Mitla*   Lohnt einen Umweg / Worth a detour

Landschaft
Landscape

★★ <u>Bar. del Cobre</u>
★★ *Popocatépetl*   Eine Reise wert / Worth a journey

★ Isla Cozumel
★ *Grutas de García*   Lohnt einen Umweg / Worth a detour

5452 ▲	Bergspitze mit Höhenangabe in Metern / Mountain top with height in meters
(2308)	Ortshöhe / Height of settlement
Parque	Nationalpark, Naturpark / National park, nature park
⊥	Kirche / Church
⊿	Kirchenruine / Church ruin
⊥	Kloster / Monastery
⊿	Klosterruine / Monastery ruin
⊥	Schloß, Burg / Palace, castle
⊿	Schloß-, Burgruine / Palace ruin, castle ruin
⁄	Wasserfall / Waterfall
∩	Höhle / Cave
∴	Ruinenstätte / Ruins
·	Sonstiges Objekt / Other object
✈	Verkehrsflughafen / Airport
✈	Flugplatz / Airfield

50 km
25 mi

Road Atlas of Mexico

*Please refer to back cover for an overview
of this Road Atlas*

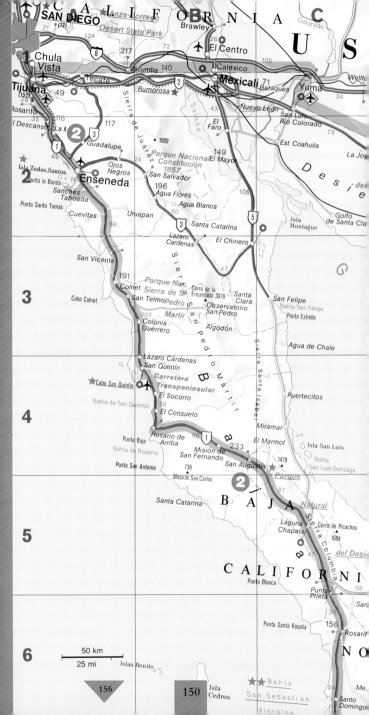

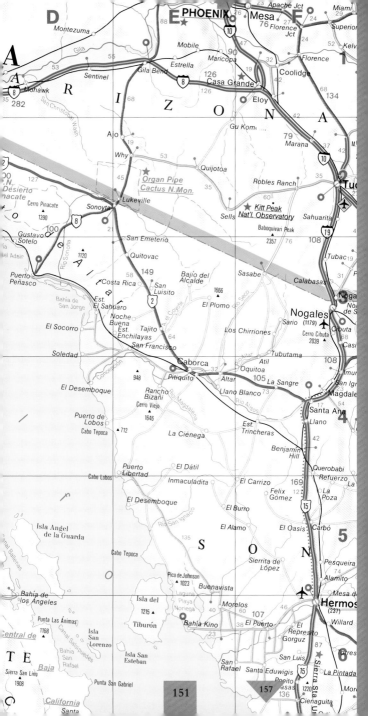

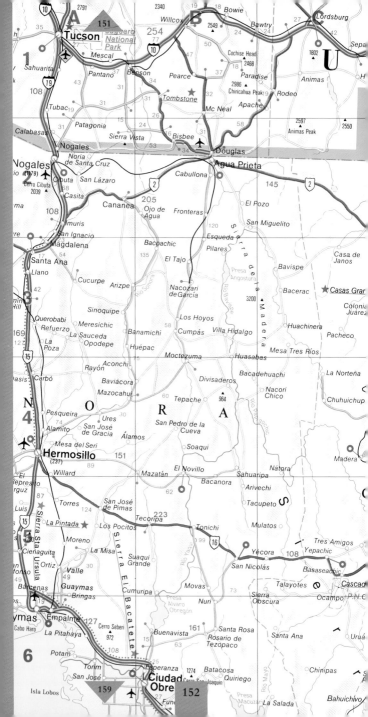

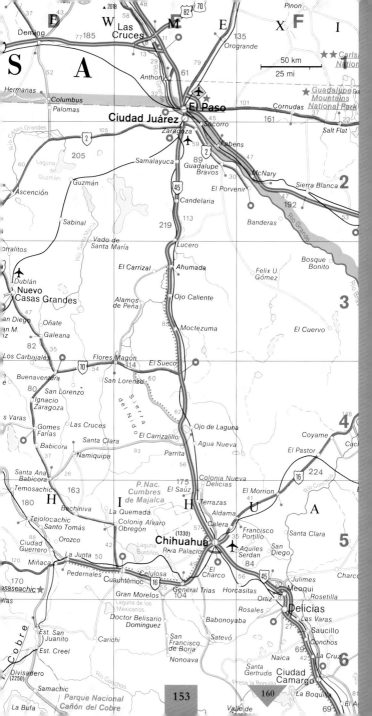

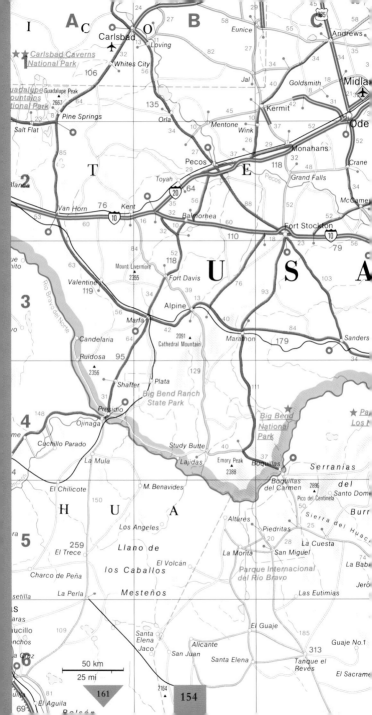

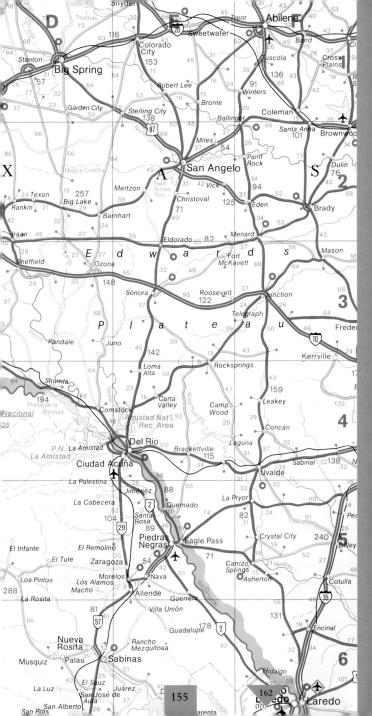

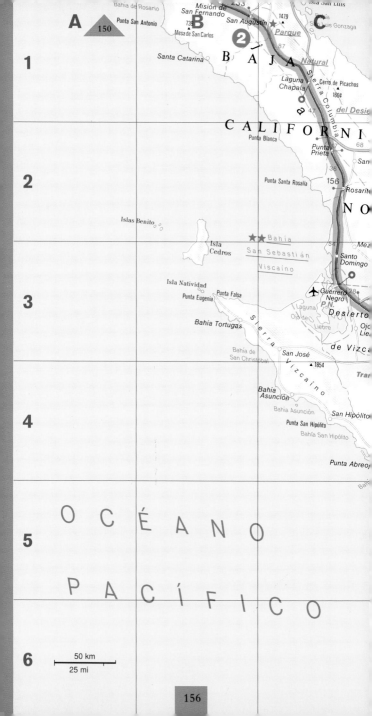

A ▲ 150   Punta San Antonio   Bahía de Rosario

Misión de San Fernando   San Agustín   Isla San Luis

B   739   Mesa de San Carlos   **2**   *Parque*

Santa Catarina   B A J A

C   San Luis Gonzaga   1479   87   *Natural*

1

Laguna Chapala   Sierra Columbia   Cerro de Picachos ▲ 1604   *del Desie*

C A L I F O R N I

Punta Blanca   Punta Prieta   68   *San*

2   Punta Santa Rosalía   156   Rosari

N O

Islas Benito

Isla Cedros   ★★ Bahía San Sebastián   Mez

Vizcaíno   Santo Domingo

3

Isla Natividad   Punta Falsa   ✈ Guerrero Negro   28

Punta Eugenia   Laguna Ojo de Liebre   P.N. Desierto

Bahía Tortugas   Sierra   Ojo de Lie

de Vizca

Bahía de San Christóbal   San José ▲ 1854   Vizcaíno   Tra

4

Bahía Asunción   Bahía Asunción   San Hipólito

Punta San Hipólito   Bahía San Hipólito

Punta Abreo

5   O C É A N O

P A C Í F I C O

6   50 km   25 mi

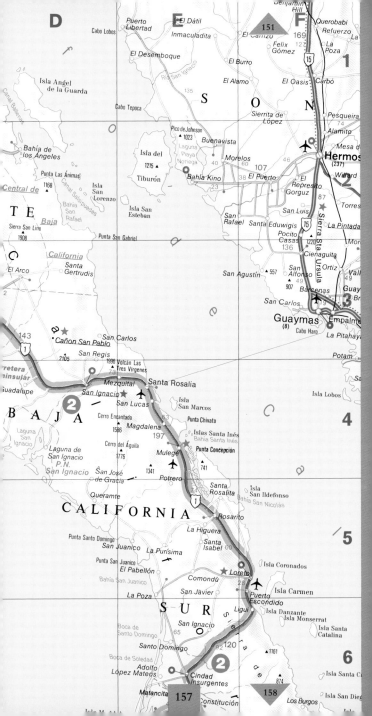

D

Cabo Lobos
Puerto
Libertad

E El Dátil
Inmaculadita

151

F
Benjamín
Hill
Querobabi Refuerzo La
169
127
La
Poza
15

1

El Desemboque
El Burro
El Álamo
El Carrizo
Félix
Gómez
El Oasis Carbó
Pesqueira
74
Alamito

Cabo Tepoca
Río San Ignacio
135

S

O

N

Mesa d

Sierrita de
López

Isla Ángel
de la Guarda

Pico de Johnson
▲ 1023

Buenavista

Isla del
1215 ▲

Tiburón

Bahía de
los Ángeles

Punta Las Ánimas
1168

Central de

Isla
San
Lorenzo

Bahía
San
Rafael

TE

Baja

Sierra San Lino
1908

Isla San
Esteban

Punta San Gabriel

California

Laguna
Playa
Noriega

Morelos
40 60
Bahía Kino
38 El Puerto
23

107 46
El
Represito
Gorguz

Hermos (237)

2

Willard

San Luis
87
Torres

La Pintada

Santa Gertrudis

San
Rafael Santa Eduwigis
Pocito
Casas
136

15

Sierra Sta Ursula

El Arco

Santa
Gertrudis

San Agustín
557

San
Alfonso
907

Ciénaguita
Ortíz

Barcenas

Val

49
Guay

San Carlos
Br

143

Cañon San Pablo
2105
San Regis

1996
▲

Volcán Las
Tres Vírgenes

Guaymas
(8) Cabo Haro

Empalme
La Pitahaya

Potam

3

retera
insular
Guadalupe

Mezquital
San Ignacio
San Lucas

Santa Rosalía

Isla Lobos

Sa

BAJA

2

Cerro Encantado
1586

Magdalena
197

Isla
San Marcos

Punta Chivato

Islas Santa Inés
Bahía Santa Inés

Isla
San Ignacio

Cerro del Águila
1776

1341

Mulegé
Punta Concepción
741

Laguna de
San Ignacio
P.N.
San Ignacio

San José
de Gracia

Potrero

Santa
Rosalita

1

Isla
San Ildefonso
Bahía San Nicolás

4

Queramte

CALIFORNIA

Rosarito

La Higuera

Santa
Isabel 60

Punta Santo Domingo
San Juanico

Punta San
Juanico

Bahía San Juanico

La Purísima
El Pabellón
La Poza

SUR

San Javier

Comondú

San Ignacio
65

Loreto

Puerto
Escondido
Ligui

Isla Coronados

Isla Carmen

Isla Danzante
Isla Monserrat

5

Boca de
Santo Domingo

Santo Domingo

Sierra de
92 120

Isla Santa
Catalina

Isla Santa Cr

Boca de Soledad

Adolfo
López Mateos

2

Cindad
Insurgentes

▲ 1161

874

Los Burgos

Isla San Die

6

Matancita
Isla M

157

Constitución

158

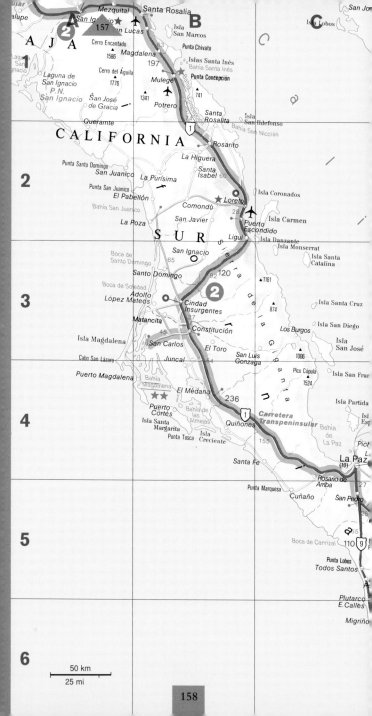

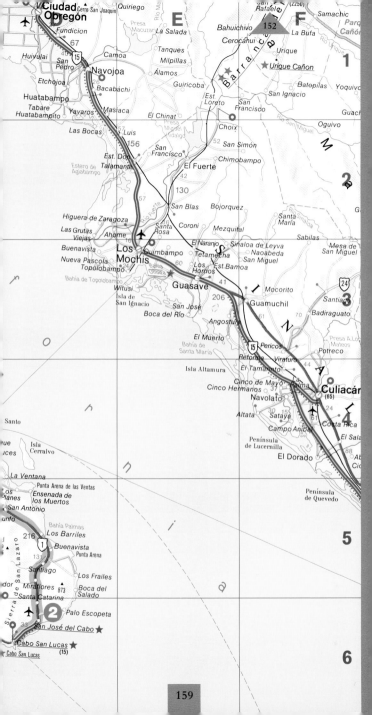

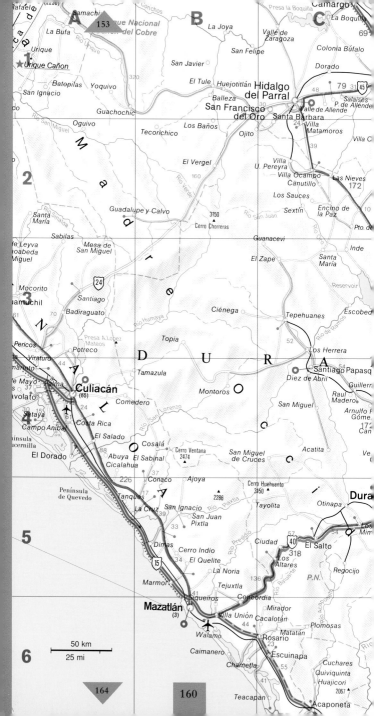

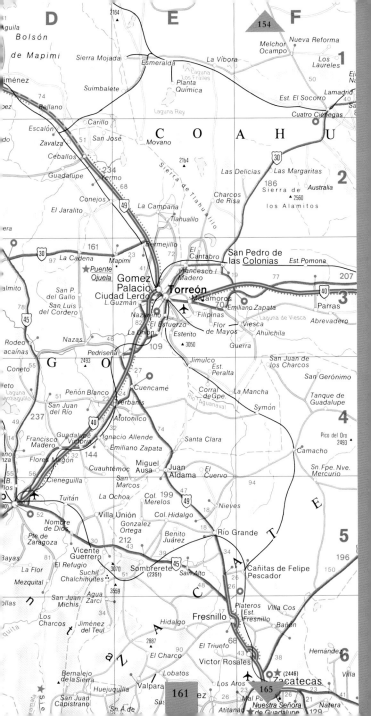

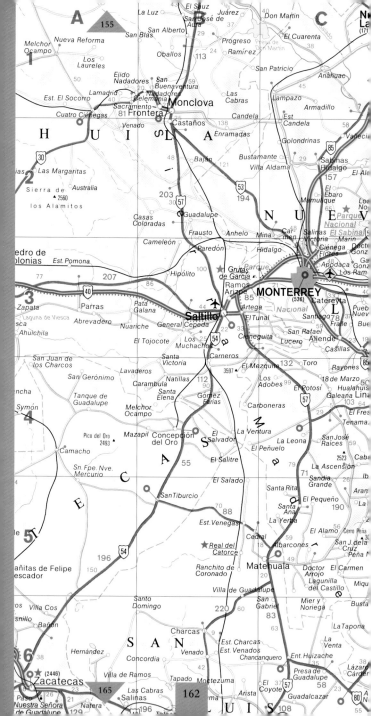

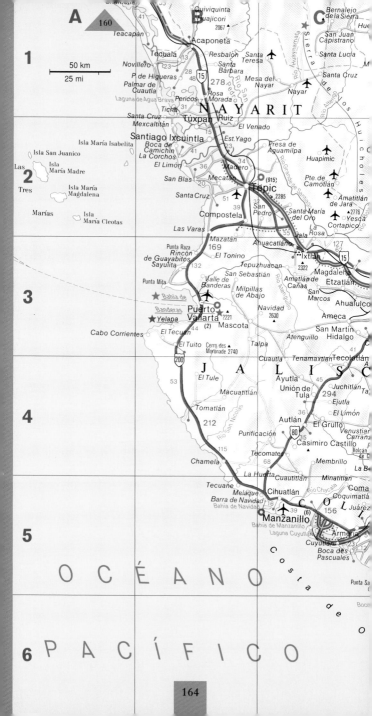

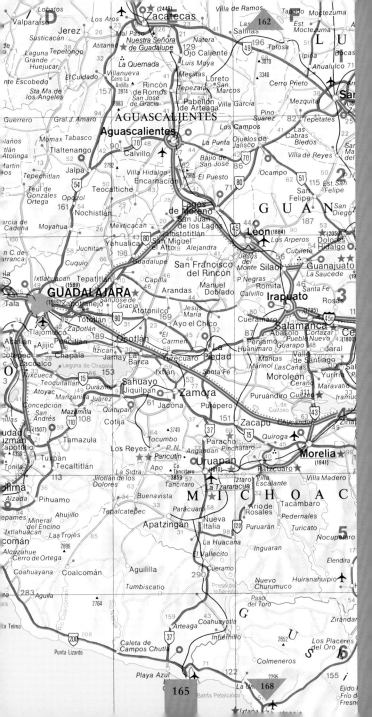

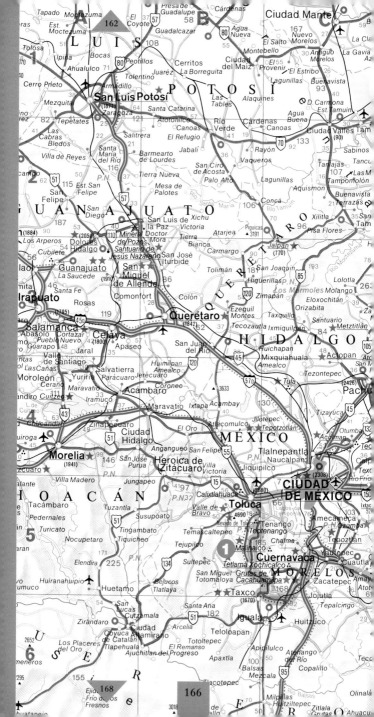

1

50 km
25 mi

G o l f o

Manuel
Cuauhtemoc 81
Lomas del Real
Colonia 34 Altamira
Ciudad
Madero
Tampico
(112)
Tampico Alto

Ebano 24 35
Reventaderos
15
onio
yón

d e

2

117 Panuco
Palmar
Prieto 38 Topila
El Higo
193
Ozuluama
(180)
70

M é x i c o

105 29
Tempoal 28
Magosal
Naranjos
Saladero
Restinga Larga
Cabo Rojo
La Laja
Isla del Idolo
Tamiahua

Tantoyuca 22
(127) 18
140 49
Alazán 35
Potrero del Llano
Tamiahua

ahualica
ali
chiatipan
uistengo
Ixhuatlán
Llano de
Emmedio
Álamo
Tihuatlán
138
Metlaltoyuca
Santiago de la Peña
Cazones
58
Barra de Tuxpan
Barra de Tamilco
Tuxpan
45

3

itlán
uayacocotla
Mecapalapa
120
Poza Rica
Tecolutla
Huehuetlán
(130)
Tajín 22
93
Papantla
Agua
Blanca 203
Xicotepec
Coyutla
Pahuatlán
Totoapa
Honey
Huauchinango
Espinal
Bolsas de
Agua
71
Nautla
Tulancingo
Yohualichán
Cuetzalán
40
Martinez
de la Torre
37
Vallarta
Tlapacoyan

4

Cuautepec
(119)
Zacatlán
Tlatlanquitepec
Misantla
122
Punta del Morro
Punta Delgada
peapulco
Chignahuapan
Tetela
Teziutlán
(1990)
Altotonga
(180)
Apam
Santa María
(229) 208
Zacapoaxtla
Jardín Lecuona
Naolinco
Punta Villa Rica
114
Perote
Xalapa (1420)
Punta Mancha
Tláxco
Cofre de Perote
El Lencero
(140)
Zempoala
Punta Zempoala
Apizaco
Atlzayanca
4292
XICO
59
José Cardel
La Antigua
TLAXCALA P.N.
Oriental
Ixhuacán
104
32
Cápaxtla
Zacatepec Chichotla
Cosautlán
Totutla
60

5

Tlaxcala La Malinche
El
Sec
Tlachichuca
P.N.
Huatusco
Veracruz
Punta Antón Liza
ojotzinga
epetl
holula
4461
Tepetlaxco
94
Citlaltépetl
Cosomatepec
(3)
Antón Lizard
tepec
Acatzingo
5700
Paso del Macho
(150)
72
Puebla
Amozoc
150
Fortín
(920)
Córdoba
Ignacio
de la Llave 88
(2162)
Tepeaca
Tecamachalco
(150)
71
Joachim
Alva
Atlixco
39
Morelos
Fortín
de las Flores
151 60
Tlacotalpan
78

U E B L A
Orizaba
Cosolapa
Acatlán
(145)
Jicaro
Acula

zúcar de
Matamoros
San
Antonio 76
P.N.
Pico de
Orizaba
Zongolica
Tierra Blanca
Cor
(190)
San Juan
Ixcaquixtla
(150)
Tehuacán
El Palmar
Nueva
Patria 94
Ciudad
Alemán
(125)
Carretera
Panamericana
58
Psa. Temaxcal
3719
79
Tesecho
utla
Coxcatlán
Presa
Miguel Alemán
Temaxcal
Tuxtepec
Lom
Bo
Acatlán 29
(125)
64
Teotitlán
Tenango
62
Villa A
(92)
148
Petlalcingo
72 23
121
Huapanapan
Huautla
Jalapa de
Díaz
Chiltepec
Pla
Vic
Ramírez
Camotlán
Pochotepec 67
215
camiba
2896
Tepel
de M
Huajuapan
de León
64
Cuicatlán
169
Mano
Marques
Tonalá
Coix
Río Grande
San Francisco
Reforma

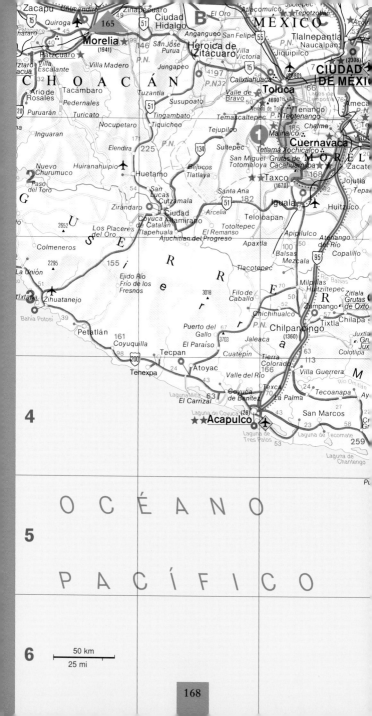

Zacapu Chirandiro Zinapécuaro El Oro Atlacomulco Jilotepec Tepotzotlán

MÉXICO

Quiroga 15 165 51 Ciudad Hidalgo B Angangueo San Felipe Tlalnepantla

Morelia (1941) San José Purua Heroica de Zitácuaro Villa Victoria Jiquipilco Naucalpan

Bátzcuaro Jungapeo 197 Calixtlahuaca **CIUDAD DE MÉXICO**

C H O A C Á N Villa Madero P.N. 15 (2980)

Ario de Rosales Tacámbaro Tuzantla Susupoato Valle de Bravo **Toluca** Ameca

Puruarán Pedernales 51 Tingambato Temascaltepec Nevado de Toluca Tenango Teotenango Chalma

Turicato Nocupetaro Tiquicheo Tejupilco P.N. Malinalco **Cuernavaca**

Inguaran 171 Sultepec Tetlama Xochicalco **M O R E L**

P.N. 225 134 San Miguel Grutas de Zacate

Nuevo Churumuco Huiranahuipio Huetamo Bejucos Tlatlaya Totomaloya Cacahuamilpa 168

G Paso del Toro San Lucas Cutzamala Santa Ana **Taxco** (1670) Jojutla Tepa

Zirándaro Ciudad Altamirano Arcelia Iguala Huitzuco

2652 Coyuca de Catalán Totoltepec

Los Placeres del Oro Tlapehuala El Remanso Apipilco Atenango del Río Copalillo

Colmeneros Ajuchitlan del Progreso Apaxtla 100 Balsas 95

2295 155 Tlacotepec Mezcala

La Unión Ejido Río Frío de los Fresnos 3018 Filo de Caballo Milpillas Zitlala Grutas de Oxto

Ixtapa Zihuatanejo r Chichihualco Zumpango Tixtla Chilapa

Bahía Potosí 39 Puerto del Gallo 3703 Jaleaca **Chilpancingo** (1360) Juxtla Colotlipa

Petatlán 161 Coyuquilla El Paraíso Cuatepin Tierra Colorada 166 Villa Guerrera **M**

200 Tecpan Atoyac Valle del Río Río Omitlan

Tenexpa Laguna Mitla El Carrizal Coyuca de Benitez Texca La Palma Tecoanapa Ay

Laguna de Coyuca **Acapulco** San Marcos 259

Laguna de Tres Palos Laguna de Tecomate

Laguna de Chantengo

O C É A N O

5

P A C Í F I C O

6 50 km / 25 mi

168

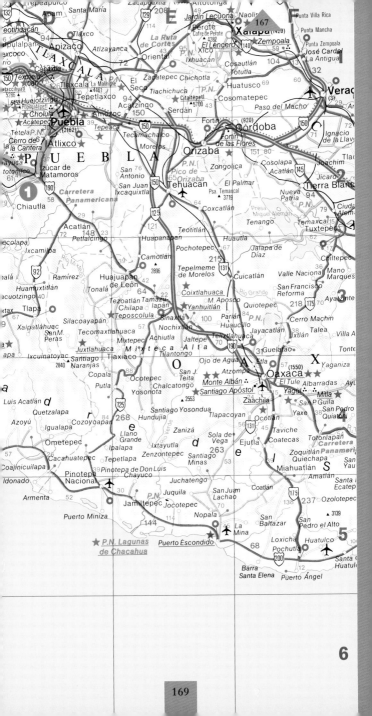

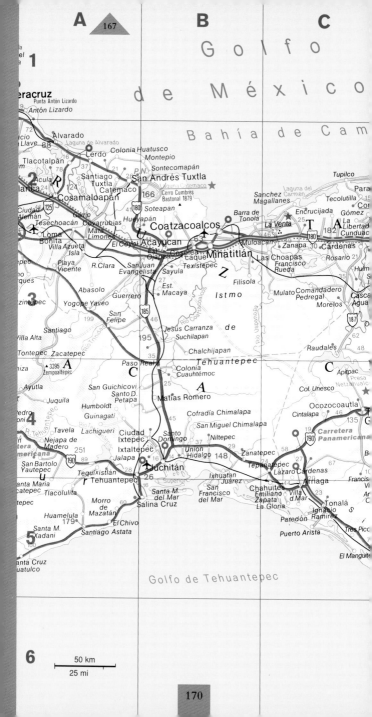

1

G o l f o

d e   M é x i c o

B a h í a   d e   C a m

2

Veracruz
Punta Antón Lizardo
Antón Lizardo
Alvarado
Colonia Huatusco
Lerdo
Montepio
Tlacotalpán
Sontecomapán
Acula
Santiago Tuxtla
San Andrés Tuxtla
Tupilco
Ciudad Alemán
Catemaco
166
Cerro Cumbres Bastonal 1879
Sanchez Magallanes
Laguna del Carmen
Tecolutilla
Cosamaloapán
Soteapan
Para
Cor
Gómez
Covarrubias
Hueyapán
Barra de Tonolá
Encrucijada
Tesechoacán
Coatzacoalcos
La Venta
Loma Bonita
El Coyol
Acayucan
Muloacan
Zanapa
Cárdenas
La Libertad
Cunduac
Villa Azueta
Isla
Mata Limones
Ojapa
Coacotla
Minatitlán
Las Choapas
Francisco Rueda
Rosario
Playa Vicente
R.Clara
San Juan Evangelista
Texistepec
Sayula
Hum
S

3

Abasolo
Est. Macaya
Filisola
Mulato
Comandadero Pedregal
Casca Agua
Yogope Yaveo
Guerrero
Istmo
Morelos
San Felipe
Jesús Carranza
Suchilapan
Santiago
Zacatepec
d e
Raudales
Tontepec
Chalchijapan
Tehuantepec
Paso Real

4

Zempoaltepec 3395
A
Colonia Cuauhtémoc
Apitpac
Presa Netzahualc
niza
Ayutla
San Guichicovi
Santo D. Petapa
A
Matías Romero
Col. Unesco
Juquila
Humboldt
Cofradía Chimalapa
San Miguel Chimalapa
Ocozocoautla
Cintalapa
Guinagati
Carretera Panamericana
Tavela
Lachiguerí
Ciudad Ixtepec
Santo Domingo
Niltepec
Nejapa de Madero
Ixtaltepec
Union Hidalgo
Zanatepec
San Bartolo Yautepec
Jalapa
Juchitán
Tepanatepec
Lázaro Cárdenas
Francis Vi
Tequixistlán
Tehuantepec
Ixhuatan Juárez
Chahuites
Arriaga
Ar
Tlacolulita
Santa M. del Mar
San Francisco del Mar
Emiliano Zapata
Villa d.Mar
Tonalá
Huamelula
Morro de Mazatán
Salina Cruz
La Gloria
Ignacio Ramirez
Tres Pico

5

Santa M. Xadani
El Chivo
Santiago Astata
Puerto Arista
El Manguite
Santa Cruz Huatulco

Golfo de Tehuantepec

6

50 km
25 mi

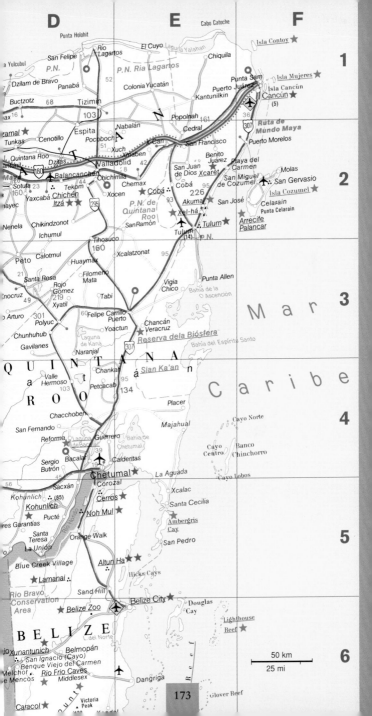

This index lists all the main sights, beaches off the beaten track and archaeological sites mentioned in this guide. Numbers in bold indicate a main entry, italics a photograph.

INDEX

What do you get for your money?

A pound is worth approx. 14 pesos, a US dollar about 9.45 pesos and a Canadian Dollar 6.40 pesos. It is advisable to bring US dollars into the country and exchange them into pesos as needed; small notes are especially useful. Owing to the high inflation, prices and exchange rates become dated rather quickly. Please note that the symbol for dollars and pesos ($) are identical!

The obligatory visit to archaeological sites and museums means spending from US $2 to $4 per person, children pay less. All churches have free admission. A 200-km first-class bus journey can cost as little as US $5, and only US $2.50 for second class. The railways are even cheaper, but much slower. In some places, it is possible to rent a VW beetle for about US $28, and the domestic flight from Mexico City to Acapulco costs about US $75. Taxis in Acapulco cost US $2 within the city and US $4 to hotels on the outskirts. In Mexico City, a ride in the city bus or underground costs only 3 pesos. The crossing from La Paz (Baja California) to Puerto Vallarta in the mainland (an 18-hour ferry journey) costs about US $75 for a double exterior cabin.

A modest accommodation can be had for US $8 per person, and a simple meal in a restaurant set you back by US $4. A beer cost between US $0.80 and US $1.25. A huge, freshly pressed glass of orange juice costs only about US $0.80 on the street.

It is very expensive to phone abroad from your hotel room, after all charges and taxes have been added; even a short call will be expensive (to Europe, no less than US $30), so it's advisable to use a phone card instead.

Prices in shops are fixed, but in the markets, streets and beaches, vendors expect you to haggle. A 15 % VAT (value added tax) is always included in your bill. When leaving the country expect to pay an airport tax of US $13 per person. In 1993, the new peso was introduced, and three zeroes were eliminated from the old one. Its symbol (N$) is not used any longer, and all coins and notes have now been replaced.

Get more out of your holiday!

Use Marco Polo Language Guides to understand and be understood

- Useful phrases for every situation
- Do's and don'ts
- Complete menus
- Travelling with kids
- Over 1000 of the most important words you're ever likely to need – plus Local Tips!

These language guides are made for you!

How to say it – communication made easy!